Put My Stuff Back!

Right Now!

Rev. Dr. Janie Watkins

© 2001 by Rev. Dr. Janie Watkins

Put My Stuff Back! Right Now!
by Rev. Dr. Janie Watkins

Printed in the United States of America
ISBN 1-931232-72-5

Short quotations or occasional page copying for personal or group study is permitted and encouraged. Permission will be granted upon written request to the author. Unless otherwise identified, all Scripture quotations are from the King James version of the Bible. Emphasis within Scripture quotes is the author's own. Please take note that the name satan and related names are not capitalized. We choose not to acknowledge him even at the risk of breaking grammatical rules.

All rights reserved. No part of this publication may be reproduced or transmitted in any form or by any means without written permission of the publisher.

Xulon Press
344 Maple Ave. West, #302
Vienna, VA 22180
703-691-7595
XulonPress.com

CONTENTS

Chapter 1 . . . . Unbroken Curses

Chapter 2 . . . . Discerning of Spirits

Chapter 3 . . . . Disarming the Devil

Chapter 4 . . . . From Foothold to Stronghold

Chapter 5 . . . . Blessed Beyond Measure

Chapter 6 . . The Presence at Work on Your Behalf

Chapter 7 . . . . He's Already Defeated

DEDICATION

I dedicate this book to my oldest sister, Dorothy D. Parker (Dottie) of Newburn, N. C. I love you sis, and I am so proud to call you, my sister. Even though we've gotten older, we still giggle when we have our talks. Thank you for being my big sister.

I dedicate this book to my grand dad, Bishop Norman B. Brown (now with the Lord). Your memory means so much to me. My life is so much the richer, because of you.

Most Lovingly, I dedicate this book to my parents, Rev. James A. Patterson, Sr., and Elder Jessie Mae Patterson (now with the Lord). My precious mom and dad, I will forever hold you so near and dear to my heart.

ACKNOWLEDGEMENTS

My life is so much the richer because of you:

Bro. Jimmie Watkins
Bro. Andre' Dandridge
Bishop Odell Fulton
Rev. Dr. George Gibson, D.D.
Dr. Frankie Gibson, Ph.D
Pastor Linda Shields
Bishop John Bowden, MD, Ph.D
Rev. Dr. Janice Bowden, Ph.D
Rev. Dr. Amos Bracheen, Ph.D
Mother Ruth McQuillar
Dr. Louise Long, D.D.
Deac. Helen Green
Dr. & Sis. Johnnie McClendon, D.D.
Sis. Angela Thomas
Pastor Jerry Hardison
Pastor & Sis. Terry Streeter
Sis. Barbara Shedrick
Pastor Frederick Gilliam
Dr. & Mrs. David London, Ph.D
Pastor Benjamin Smith, Sr.
Rev. Kathryn Torres
Elder & Rev. Robert Harrington
Sis. Yvonne Woodson

Prophetess Sheila Williams
Dr. Mary Washam, Ph.D
Pastor Gladys Willis
Pastor Catherine Young
Min. & Sis. Henry Walker
Min. Carolyn Boston
Min. Mary Chambers
Rev. Barbara Faison
Dr. James Sturdivant, Sr. D.D.
Sis. Ann Starr
Missionary Dorothy McMiller
Pastor Shirley Daniels
Evg. Gwendolyn Fisher
Evg. Deborah Drysden
Pastor & Sis. Alexander Jones
Evg. Mary Brown
Rev. Dorothy Smith
Rev. Mildred Hughes
Pastor Sylvia Earls
Pastor & Sis. Paul Brown, Sr.
Rev. Estelle Martin
Rev. Cassandra James
Sis. Mary McQuillar

Dr. Annie Barksdale, Ph.D
Min. Delia Adams
Pastors Jack & Deena Casion
Pastor Rosa Lindsey
Pastor Sarah Stevenson
Pastor Elizabeth Sears
Rev. Ronald Patterson
Min. Kecia DeCosta
Pastor & Sis. J. C. Elmore
Rev. Linda Garrett
Pastor Dorothy Harper
Bishop O'shea Granger
Pastor Lula Howard
Min. Sharon Stephens
Evg. Edith McKeller
Sis. Dorothy Mangum

Prophetess Jacquelyn Godbold
Min. Sarah Lee
Deacon Leroy Lee
Elder Deborah Jones
Evg. Esther Lindsey Peake
Pastor Curtis Redmond
Evg. Deborah Burns
Evg. Ethel Driessen
Evg. Josie Kendall
Min. Wayne Roach
Sis. Christine Stuart
Pastor Carrie Williams
Rev. Jennie Mae Williams
Prophetess Brenda Todd
Evg. Liticia Johnson
Evg. Geneva Maxwell

FOREWORD

As embarrassing as it is, we must take the blame for allowing our stuff to have fallen in satan's hands. God gave us dominion over the earth, and we have faltered to failure in our rule! That being said, now is the time to be relentless in our mission to reclaim it." . . .the kingdom of heaven suffereth violence, and the violent take it by force" (St. Matthew 11:12). Whoever, whatever, whenever, however, wherever, resolve that nothing will stand between you and the blessings that are yours through the eternal victory won by Jesus Christ!

In "Put My Stuff Back!!! Right Now!!!!," Dr. Janie Watkins gives instructions on how to annihilate our enemy and walk in our anointing. This powerful guide will empower, encourage, and inspire you. Read it, and prepare to assume the position. What position? The position to receive the blessings that breaking the curses and disarming the enemy will usher in, first to shower you, then to bathe you, and finally to overtake you!!!

In HIM,

Dr. George Gibson, Jr.
Shepherd
Christian Love Worship Center

CHAPTER 1

UNBROKEN CURSES

Yes, I am Violent and I am TAKING MY STUFF BACK. ALL OF IT!!!

And if you know what I know, you will take yours back too. Your what?

Everything satan stole from you. Go get it! Go slap him around just for GP and take your stuff back.

Guess what? satan has your stuff and he also have plans to take your children's stuff, and your grandchildren and your great grandchildren's stuff and many more generations after them. You see, I found out the devil mimics God. Remember what he said in Isaiah 14:14, let's go there: " *I will ascend above the heights of the clouds; I will be like the Most High.*" But we know he can not be like God. he is the creature. (satan) How can the creature be like it's Creator? The only way he can is to accept Jesus as Lord and we know good and well the defeated one is not going to do that.

God is a generational God. If you don't obey Him when He has called you to Ministry, He'll go right down your lineage and find Him somebody that will go. He's not going to be short-changed because of your disobedience. I said all that to say this: If God is a generational God (and He is), then the defeated one is a generational devil. he did say he will be like the Most High.

You see in that Scripture also, the defeated one had to Reverence God as the "Most High."

Now to get back to this generational thing, there are generational curses in some of our lives that are still not broken. And if they're not broken they will go on and on and on. But your enemy "MUST" be stopped and you're going to have to do it.

There are inherited curses that have not been broken which have given satan territorial rights.

This reminds me when I was in Real Estate Law class, and we were studying on Squatters Rights. And we came across this scenario: If you had property that someone was squatting in, and you did nothing openly or publicly to stop them from living there. Well if that squatter lived there for a period of twenty one years, that property is then legally his. Also, if that squatter stayed there for let's say a period of ten years, and decided to leave, but he told a family member or friend about the property and they came and stayed there for another eleven years. Well, the original squatter can come back and claim the property as his. The law calls this, "Tacking On." The original squatter tacked on the other squatter's years to his and he went and file to be owner.

This is what the devil does. he occupies the house (mind) of an unsaved person until there's a strong hold there, then he calls for his other demons to tack on. Let me share something with you, the devil HATES YOU! Simply because he knows what you are getting ready to come in to. Yes, he knows about your inheritance of eternal life. Trust me, he has seen your Mansions in Glory and he has seen your Crowns and the Jewels in your Crowns. If he can stop you and take all, not only what's promised to you here, but what you will inherit in Glory, he'll take it. But you must get violent and TAKE, TAKE, TAKE, all that he has taken from you here. Go after what's yours! You just don't let anyone take something that belong to you and let them get by with it. You see, the devil took my son from me and I have a Vendetta against him. I often tell people, I go after satan with a vengeance because of what he has done. Not only for what he has done, but for what he is doing even now in my family. I will not let the enemy rest. The only time he gets any rest is when I go to sleep because when I wake up, he's in for war! I have made a vow to do my part in educating this world about their enemy.

What is a curse?

A prayer or invocation for harm to come upon someone; to call upon divine or supernatural power to send harm or injury to someone. To bring great evil upon someone.

The purpose of a curse is to cause destruction or

death. Jesus said, "satan comes but to steal, kill, and destroy." The Old Testament is full of Scriptures that reference curses. One of the reasons Christ Jesus died was so we could be set free from such evil. We were given power in Jesus' Name to break every type of evil there is.

We've got to know how to fight our enemy. Remember he is spirit. You don't fight a spiritual enemy with natural weapons. (II Cor. 10:4), *"For the weapons of our warfare are not carnal, but mighty through God for the pulling down of strongholds.* So many Christians are defeated as I write this book. So many are defeated for lack of knowledge. When you are walking with people that are not knowledgeable, it calls for caution. (Hosea 4:6) *My people are destroyed for lack of knowledge; because you have rejected knowledge; I will also reject thee that thou shalt be no priest to me, seeing thou hast forgotten the law of thy God, I will also forget thy children."* So you see, we must get knowledge especially of our enemy. I am not saying to be pre-occupied with thoughts of him, but just be aware, alert, focused. Be acutely aware of one who wants to destroy you and all that you are about. God has called us to wisdom. (Eccl. 7:12). *"For wisdom is a defense as money is a defense but the excellence of knowledge is that wisdom gives life to those who have it."*

God does not want us to be ignorant of the devices or strategies of the defeated one. (II Cor. 2:11) *"Lest satan should get an advantage of us; for we are not ignorant of his devices."*

If the Body of Christ continues in sin, the Holy Scriptures clearly states that we will suffer and eventually be taken into captivity. Most Christians that are constantly going through, often wonder why they can't seem to get away from the "same" problems. It's because of ignorance to the knowledge of what is happening to them. God wants us to not just go from day to day, just skipping along unaware of the evil devices of the devil.

We are responsible for what we know and we're responsible for what we don't know also. I've often heard people say, "God is so loving, He won't hold me responsible for what I don't know." Well, I have you know, God does not excuse us. We are responsible and God holds us accountable for what He has already spoken in His Word. (Lev. 5:17), *"And if a soul sin and commit any of these things which are forbidden to be done by the Commandments of the Lord; though he wist it not, yet he is guilty, and shall bear his iniquity."* We are responsible and will be held accountable . God said, "In the last days knowledge will cover the earth." It's no excuse to be without knowledge when it's slapping you in your face everyday. Like I mentioned earlier, (*Hosea* 4:6), if we don't read and study God's Word, we are rejecting knowledge.

Jesus sent the Holy Spirit back to us to help us with knowledge and everything else. But, especially knowledge. He (the Holy Spirit) is the Paraclete, our helper. He is the one sent to walk along side of us to help us. If we've sinned and forgotten to repent, (which opens doors to demonic powers), He will bring that back to our memory so we can Confess it before God and Repent of it. In fact, that's part of His Dossier. He is a Revealer. Ask the Holy Spirit to reveal any and all curses operative in your life. He will do just that. And when He reveals, you will know how to pray and come against the defeated one.

Often times, no matter how much we pray about a situation, it appears that the enemy has the upper hand anyway. Remember I said, "It Appears." But in actually, when this does happen, it's because there are unbroken curses that are yet prevailing in your life. God wants us with knowledge of the Holy and the unholy. (Eze.44:23) " They shall teach my people the difference between the Holy and the unholy, and cause them to discern between the unclean and the clean.

Most Christians are not even slightly aware of some things in their homes which enable curses to operate freely in their lives. I mentioned this in my book, "It's My Time To Be Blessed." From time to time, the Holy Spirit have me to take Inventory of what's in my home. I throw out some things that should not be there. Even some mail. Oh yes, mail. Oh you'd be surprised.

Please be aware also that there are curses from God as well as satan. Curses sent from God are for the sole purpose of getting the person to turn from his wicked ways and turn back to God. curses sent by satan are for destruction. When satan sends curses, he sends his demons to specific people, or a specific family line for a specific purpose. his demons make sure the curse is carried out.

Sources of curses

Yes, there are sources of curses. Sins of forefathers, being involved in unclean and unholy things, walking on satan's battlegrounds, living on cursed land, house paintings. Some demonic spirits even attach themselves to animals. Remember when Jesus cast them out of the man and they asked if they could go into the swine? devils don't change! Another source is eating food that has been offered or sacrificed to devils. When we break vows to God, (disobedience to God), this leaves a door open to curses as well.

Remember when God told Joshua to take Jericho, He was specific. He told them not to touch the goods in Jericho. He was specific about this. But as you know the story, they disobeyed God. (Josh. 7:1), *" But the children of Israel committed a Trespass regarding accursed things, for Achan , the son of Carmi, the son of Zabdi, the son of Zorah, of the Tribe of Judah, took the accursed thing; so the anger of the Lord burned against the children of*

Israel." The other people were not aware that Achan had sinned. No one knew except Almighty God and satan. Even Joshua didn't understand. He thought that God brought them over Jordan to destroy them by delivering them into the hands of the Amorites. Joshua starts to pray and cry out to the Lord. *God said, " Get up from there Joshua. Get up off of your face! The bottom line is, Israel has sinned and they have transgressed my Covenant which I commanded them: for they have taken of the accursed thing, and have stolen and dissembled also, and they have put it even among their own stuff.* God told them, *" I will not be with you until you destroy the accursed thing from among you."*

If God will not be with you, guess who will? Guess who then have free reign in your life? You guessed it, satan. Our God is Holy and He requires Holiness and Obedience. Where there is sin and disobedience, satan has free reign to do what he does best. Did you notice that Achan had plenty of room to repent, but he still didn't. Because he didn't repent, Joshua, at the command of God, took Achan and the stuff, I want you to see something in this; because Achan sinned, his sons and daughters were stoned to death. Yes, God revisited the sins of the fathers on the children. They died because of their daddy's sins. Achan bought a curse not only on himself, but on his house by being disobedient and touching the accursed thing. So, we must be mindful that we don't give the devil any foot hold to come in.

Keep in mind, if you walk Holy before the Lord of Glory, you have authority over the devil and his house. (Luke 10:19), *"Behold, I give unto you power to tread on serpents and scorpions, and over all the power of the enemy: and nothing shall by any means hurt you. (Mark 16:17-18), " And these signs shall follow them that believe in my name; shall they cast out devils; they shall speak with new tongues; they shall take up serpents; and if they drink any deadly thing, it shall not hurt them; they shall lay hands on the sick, and they shall recover.*

We have been given power and authority over the enemy, but power and authority means nothing if you don't walk in it! God expects us to walk in what He gave us. You see, God knows the evil one, and He knows the depth of his evil. So, He gave us power and authority over that devil.

Inherited Curses

Curses are passed down from generation to generation. As I said earlier, the defeated one is a generational devil. Some of what you're experiencing, has been passed down to you. There are some curses that have been placed on an entire family line. satan is so evil, it's his desire to destroy entire family lines. I worked on this job, and the manager was forty one years old. She suddenly started having real bad problems with her nerves.

Well after talking with her, I realized her mother, grandmother, and great- grandmother had the same problems when they forty one. So, not only does the devil attack the family line, he also have a "set time" to turn up the heat in his destruction.

I noticed in my family there are a lot of divorces. The women are left to take care of everything. A few years ago, the Holy Spirit told me to get with my Mom, and a cousin of mine that was a generation under my mom, and myself, and one person in the generation after me. And we were to get together and pray and repent and speak into the lives of the generations after us in order to break that curse. It was always divorce, divorce, divorce. God is concerned about our lineage. (Deut. 6:6-7), *" And these words which I command you today shall be in your heart. You shall teach them diligently to your children, and shall talk of them when you sit in your house, when you walk by the way, when you lie down, and when you rise up."* (Ex. 20:5), *"For I the Lord your God am a jealous God, visiting the iniquity of the fathers upon the children to the third and fourth generation of those who hate me."*

God is clearly concerned about our lineage. You know what? God makes it clear how we can break a curse that's in our family line. (Lev. 26:40-42), *"If they shall confess the iniquity of their fathers, with their trespass which they trespassed against me, and that also they have walked contrary unto me: And that I also have walked contrary unto them and have brought them into the land of their enemies; If then their uncircumcised hearts be humbled and they then accept of the punishment of their iniquity: Then will I remember my Covenant with Jacob, and also my Covenant with Isaac, and also my Covenant with Abraham, will I remember; and I will remember the land."*

We have to deal with curses, we cannot just let sleeping dogs lie. The sins of our forefathers will indeed affect our lives unless we bring them to Jesus.

Notice in Old Testament times, every time Israel came into a revival, it was always due to their confessing and repenting of their sins and the sins of their forefathers. (Neh.9:1-3), *"Now, on the twenty-fourth day of this month, the children of Israel were assembled with fasting and sack cloth and with earth upon them. And the seed of Israel separated themselves from all strangers and stood and confessed their sins and the iniquities of their fathers. And they stood up in their place, and read the book of the law of the Lord their God, one fourth part of the day, and another fourth part they confessed, and worshiped the Lord their God."*

Scripture reference shows that God always honored

such a prayer and brought revival back to Israel.

Satan knows the principle of heritage/lineage. And he also knows that most Christians have lost the concept of heritage/lineage. All too often, he does much damage in this area. (lack of knowledge). When there are still unconfessed and unrepented sins of our forefathers, satan has a legal right to the family line. That's why there are families that most of their deaths are the same. (Cancer, liver diseases, heart attacks etc.). Or, you may find the great- grandfather was a drug addict, the grandfather, now the father, and you may see traits in the son. The devil loves the blood line. Somebody better start looking at these curses!!! This is quite clear. You would have to ignore this on purpose to not see it! We must confess the sins of our forefathers and repent of them, and break that stronghold the enemy has on the blood line. Then ask God to close that "door" so those devils can not come back.

Believe it or not, there are some curses that actually comes from God. Remember in I Chron. 21, when David committed a Trespass? (I *Chron.* 21:1), " *and satan stood up against Israel and provoked David to "number" Israel. And David said to Joab and to the rulers of the people, Go number (count) Israel from Beersheba even to Dan; and bring the number of them to me, that I may know it. And Joab answered, the Lord make His people an hundred times so many more as they be: but, my lord the king, are they not all my lord's servants? Why then doth my lord require this thing? Why will he be a cause of trespass to Israel?" Joab went ahead and counted Israel, all except Levi and Benjamin. He came back to David and gave him a report of the number of the people.* But the Word of God says, that this displeased God that David had Israel counted. Keep in mind, in Genesis, God kept telling Abraham that his seed would be innumerable, yet David attempted to do what God said was impossible to do. Because David committed this trespass, God cursed Israel. Some may say He judged Israel, but I say, He cursed Israel. And this curse was not to be broken. This curse would be carried out, why, because, the Word of God was backing it. David realized his sins and repented. (I *Chron.* 21:8), "*And David said unto God, I have sinned greatly, because I have done this thing: but now, I beseech thee, do away the iniquity of thy servant; for I have done very foolishly.*"

God forgave David, but David's sins resulted in Israel being cursed. Israel inherited a curse from God because of David's sins. (I *Chron.* 21:9), "*And the Lord spake unto Gad, David's seer, saying, Go and tell David saying, Thus saith the Lord, I offer thee three things: Choose thee one of them, that I may do it unto thee. So Gad came to David, and said unto him, Thus saith the Lord, choose thee either three years of famine; or three months to be destroyed before thy foes, while that the sword of thine enemies over taketh thee; or else three days the sword of the Lord, even the pestilence* (incurable diseases) *in the land and the angel of the Lord destroying throughout all the coasts of Israel. Now therefore, advise thyself what word I shall bring again to him that sent me. And David said unto Gad, I am in a great strait:* (between a rock and a hard place) *Let me fall now into the hand of the Lord, for very great are His mercies: but let me not fall into the hand of man.*" So the Lord sent pestilence upon Israel: and there fell of Israel, seventy thousand (70,000) men. That was one curse that could not be broken. Sometimes, we forget about the consequences of our sins. God forgives, but you are going to pay for that sin.

(Gen. 13:16), *"And I will make thy seed as the dust of the earth: so that if a man can number the dust of the earth, then shall thy seed also be numbered.*

(Gen. 16:10), *"And the angel of the Lord said unto her, I will multiply thy seed exceedingly, that it shall not be numbered for multitude.*

(Gen 32:12), *" And thou saidst, I will surely do thee good, and make thy seed as the sand of the sea, which cannot be numbered for multitude."*

(Gen. 22:17-18), *" That in blessing I will bless thee, and in multiplying I will multiply thy seed as the stars of heaven (Innumerable), and as the sand which is upon the seashore; and thy seed shall possess the gate of his enemies. And in thy seed, shall all the nations be blessed; because thou hast obeyed my voice."* You see, God made a covenant with Abraham, and "in that covenant" God mentioned that Abraham's seed would be too numerous to number. Yet, David attempted to prove God wrong and that he "COULD" count Abraham's seed. This is awesome on the mind, God placed anger in Joab so he would not attempt to get a total count. First of all, he only counted the men of war, and secondly, he still didn't count Levi and Benjamin. (I *Chron.* 21:5-6), " *And Joab gave the sum of the number of the people unto David. And all they of Israel were a thousand thousand and an hundred thousand men that drew the sword; and Judah was four hundred and seventy thousand men that drew the sword. But Levi and Benjamin counted he not among them; for the king's word was abominable to Joab.*

So, again, do you see what I mean about inherited curses? You can inherit a curse in more ways than one.

Curses of dedication

Have you been dedicated to satan by ancestors? You may have and don't know anything about it. Remember when Jesus was standing before Pilate, and hey, let's go to the Word on this one. (Mt. 27:24-25), " *When Pilate saw that he could prevail nothing, but that rather a tumult was made, he took water and washed his hands before the multitude, saying; "I am innocent of the blood of this just person, see you did it. Then answered all the people and said, His blood be on us and on our children."* Lord God! They asked that a blood line curse be on them "and" on their children. From then even until now, the Blood of Jesus Christ has been upon them.

A person of Jewish decent that accept Christ as Savior, should repent of the sins of his/her forefathers and also ask God to remove that generational curse from their family line.

Have you ever wondered why drug addict parents have drug addict children? I grant you that this is a learned behavior, but it is also an inherited sin, thus an inherited curse. We must ask the Holy Spirit (He is the revealer), to reveal to us the sins of our forefathers so that we can confess them and repent of them, so that the curse on them can be broken thus ending the patterns for generations following. As I mentioned in my book, "It's My Time To Be Blessed" the Holy Spirit have me taking inventory from time to time of my home. Some things "must" go. Anything that is contrary to the Word of God, must go. Any object that has been dedicated to satan or has an idol god image on it, on jewelry with occultic symbols on it is cursed. Be careful when you travel, especially in other countries. We often buy jewelry or souvenirs with demonic symbols on it. We buy things unaware of their meanings.

I was in a thrift store and saw these wooden sticks. They had carved images or faces on them. I bought them to put them in my plant pots, to have the vine of the plant twist around the stick. I thought it would be neat. Well, the Peace of God always dwelt in my home. My spirit is very sensitive to the things of the spirit, whether good or evil. As soon as I entered in my front door with those sticks, I felt an unsettling in my spirit. I couldn't put my finger on it right away, but I knew something was wrong. But one day I was watering my plants, and for some reason, I took a long look at the faces on the sticks. Then I realized that they were faces of idol gods or demonic images. We must be focused to the things of the Holy Spirit.

Another story I want to share with you. A friend of mine is from India. She went to the Middle East, and when she returned, she had a gift for me. This gift was a brass plaque. I adored it. Some time later, the Holy Spirit said, "Look at it." I did look at it. And there was an image of an idol. Under this god's feet was a baby crawling. Around the baby's neck was a serpent. This baby didn't stand a chance. The Holy Spirit said, "Get that out of this house." I did just that. I didn't give it to anyone, I just trashed it.

We must be aware of the strategies of our enemy. Anything that has been dedicated to satan or his demons, they consider them to be holy unto themselves. satan has a legal right to go where his stuff is. And, he has a legal right to curse the person that has his stuff. We are not to walk in fear, but we are to walk in wisdom and walk in line with the Word of God.

We are to not honor devils. Friends of mine visited Jerusalem (I have never been there, but will visit this year). During their tour there, they visited the dome of the rock. This is the muslim mosque. I am told, as you enter the mosque, you must take your shoes off. Taking your shoes off is an act of honoring allah, the demonic god of the muslims. This mosque has been dedicated to this demon god. This god mimicked Almighty God when Moses was on Mount Horeb. When God told Moses to put off his shoes. Let's go there. (Ex. 3:5), " *And He said, draw not nigh hither: put off thy shoes from off thy feet for the place whereon thou standest is* Holy Ground. " Moses took his shoes off in honor and reverence to God. But do you see this thing? Do you see how the devil imitates God? Stay Focused!

Trespassing on satan's property

The unclean thing is satan's property. God said, "Touch not the unclean thing." We must be acutely mindful where we go and what we touch. Even the world is aware of touching. There was a movie out, and the movie showed people walking down the street. And, occasionally bump into someone or may accidentally touch someone. When actual physical contact was made, that person's spirit would transfer to the other person. Movie? Yes! Reality? Yes!!! Just like that, demonic influence can transfer. Be Focused! (I *Peter* 5:8), " *Be sober, be vigilant, because your adversary the devil, walks like a roaring lion seeking whom he may devour."* he is seeking. Do you know what that word "seek" means? It means search, and when you search, you leave no stone unturned. This is how diligent your enemy is. he "study's" you. That's why he and his devils are called familiar spirits. they make sure they are familiar with you. Your ways, your habits, your likes, your dislikes, places you like to go.

they don't know your thoughts, but they plant thoughts in your mind and watch your reactions. If you react to the thought, then they know they got your attention and can pretty much tell what your next move will be. they become familiar with you.

satan is territorial. I don't care how Holy you are, I don't care how much you pray, if you have any stuff that belongs to the defeated one, he has a legal right to come where his stuff is. If you have furniture in storage, you are given a key. This key represent your authority to go where your stuff is. This is why we must be Sober and Focused. Not being pre-occupied with thoughts of the defeated one, but walking in the Wisdom of God. Just recently, I attended a Women's Ministry Conference in Maryland. In my hotel room, I noticed on the corners of the door in the bathroom, there were little stars etched in the wood. I called my girlfriend in to look at it, and we realized they were not pentagrams but just stars. Still thank God for the awareness.

Most Christians walk around La-De-Da-In and not Watching. Jesus said we are to Watch as well as Pray because your adversary is real and he's seeking who he can devour. That word "devour" really means to destroy. satan is "deadly serious" about destroying us. Yall better wake up! My brother, my sister, you better open your eyes! The devil is real. he is spirit. When we declare war on him, we fight in the spiritual realm.

Someone I know told me that someone set a curse on her. And, I asked her did she seek God about it. Her answer was, "I sent the curse back to the person that sent it to me, and I sent it back double." I told her what she did is not Godly. She argued of course, but I told her she was working witch craft. What she did is in direct contrast with what Jesus said we are to do concerning our enemies. (Luke 6:27-28), " *But I say unto you which hear, love your enemies, do good to them which hate you, bless them that curse you, and pray for them which despitefully use you.*"

It is clear that Jesus goes against the teaching of sending back curses. curses are composed of demon spirits. If you send a curse back, you are sending demons to people. And, if that's not witch craft, then I don't know what is.

If you are a TRUE Christian, a TRUE Worshiper of Jesus Christ, you shouldn't be working witch craft. You see, all of this stuff keeps you in bondage, unblessed, in fact, cursed. And if you're cursed, you're in bondage and need to be set free. How can you take your stuff back from the evil one if you're in bondage. Bondage means that your hands are tied by the devil. So, instead of you being in the position to bind him, he has you bound. So now, he got "you" and your "stuff." Hey sis, bro, get in position to go get your stuff back. Go get your mate, your health, your deliverance, your children, your anointing, your home, your car. Call them from the four winds of the earth. Go get it!!!!!!! Don't forget, the devil knows if you have power over him or not. Remember again, the seven sons of sceva???

Cursed Gifts

I just want to share something with you. People that are evil knows how to get curses into the hands of Christians, and that's by giving gifts or money etc. As the Christian accepts the money/gift, a spirit of poverty or destruction is activated in the life of that Christian. Not only in that Christian's life, but also in that family line. My sister, my brother we must be Focused, we must be Focused!

Often times when we are receiving gifts, we are not thinking about being focused - we just want the gift. But the evil one is cunning. We must listen to the voice of the Holy Spirit and when He tells us not to accept a gift, we better listen to Him! He is the God who sees. And He knows the move of the devil. He see what we can't see. Hear me Child of the Most High God, do not take satan for granted, he is the formidable foe that has your stuff. And, in many cases, he has your mama's stuff, your grandmama's stuff, and your great-grandmama's stuff. Somebody better stop the curse. Seek God in how and what you are to do in order to take it back. You see, we don't know how to pray as we ought. But God the Holy Ghost, will show us how to pray, He will give us the words to say. And, He will give us the words to speak into the lives of our descendants after us.

If you treat satan lightly, you become vulnerable to his attacks. We can't stand against the devil in our own power, Jesus enables us to stand against him. That's what "Grace" is all about. Most of the time, we hear that Grace is God's unmerited favor and this is true. But there are many Graces that He gave us. He enabled us to do what we have to do.

CHAPTER 2

DISCERNING OF SPIRITS

Yes, discernment is the mark of spiritual maturity. We are to have eyes to see and ears to hear what the Spirit of the Lord is saying to the Church. Discernment is seeing and hearing. The Holy Spirit not only speaks through the Word of God, He speaks through visions, dreams, and His Prophetic Words. But keep in mind, the Holy Spirit is in direct harmony with Jesus Christ. He will "Never" say anything contrary to the Word of God that is already written.

Discerning is not judging. Once we kill our desire to judge, then True Discerning can take place. Jesus has said, (St. John 12:47-b), " *I did not come to judge the world, but to save the world.*" Discernment is one of the Three Revelation Gifts, to perceive what is in the spirit. It's nature is to see into the nature of that which is "Veiled." Often times, instead of discerning, people judge, and you can see right through that. Jesus said, (Mt. 7:1-5), "*Judge not, that ye be not judged. For with what judgement ye judge, ye shall be judged: with what measure ye mete, it shall be measured to you again. And why beholdest thou the mote that is in thy brother's eye, but consider not the beam that is in thine own eye? Thou hypocrite, first cast out the beam out of thine own eye; and then thou shalt see clearly to cast out the mote out of thy brother's eye.*"

There are many folks in the Body walking around judging people and calling it discernment. When we judge others, we're only seeing our own image in others (Mirror image). Jesus calls a judgemental person a hypocrite. If we are to walk in true discernment, our hearts must be quite before our God. And, we must learn how to listen and wait on God. (Ps. 46:10), "*Be still and know that I am God.*" True discernment comes through a heart that's quiet before our God, not a heart that's constantly striving. Peace must rule our hearts in order for us to discern the move of God and the move of the evil one. God is looking for a Tranquil heart. (Eccl. 4:6), " *Better is a handful with quietness than both the hands full with travail and vexation of spirit.*"

Discernment comes as we are sensitive to Jesus. Discernment comes from much love for God's people.

I'm sharing all of this with you so you can know what type of spirit the devil sent to you and in that, you will know how to approach a situation in prayer. We must first access the problems. Then we learn what type of demons we're dealing with. Because in accessing the problems, there we find the nature of the spirit that's behind it all. Once you know the nature of the evil spirit you're dealing with, the war is on!!!!

Hear me please! Before you go casting out devils, be sure the fruit of the Spirit (the character of Jesus) is formed in your heart. If the character of Jesus is not formed in us, conflict will not cease.

Be aware of tricks of the enemy. If you are not aware, he will have you constantly focused on him and his demons. Our highest call is to be focused, but on Jesus only. The devil is the greatest distractor, distracting us from Jesus. But again, stay Focused on Jesus!

In this book, we are exposing the devil for who he is. He is a fault finder. When he is exposed for who he is, he moves on, but for a season. Keep that in mind, he moves on for a season. But even so, still don't break your focus on Jesus.

Remember who you're fighting. he is the accuser of the brethren. he finds fault with us and then takes it to God. he finds fault and then takes it to the Pastor. he finds fault and then takes it to the president of the Pastor's aide, and on and on and on. The defeated one loves to point the finger. When a finger is pointed at someone, there are three more fingers pointed back at the pointer. Isn't that something? Often times a fault finder sees a mirror image of themselves. But we are to replace fault finding with prayer and love. Fault finding is a strong hold and it must be dealt with. satan has a glimpse into the Ministry that God has placed in your hands. And, you can be sure that he will slow you up or even stop you if he can. You see, what Ministry does is expose him to be the devious devil that he is.

So, why should he let you make him look like the fool he is? This is warfare. And, you can tell when he has declared all out war against you because adversity will come to you from every direction. But always keep at the forefront of your mind: Your Ministry, is not your ministry. It's God's. The enemy knows this better than you and I. You see, the devil's aim is to snare God before the world, through us. And, also, to show God that He can not trust us to carry out His Ministry. So, satan will use someone sitting right there next to you in the pulpit to tear you down, to cause you to feel inadequate so you will let ministry go. Thus, many that would be delivered through your ministry, would go un-delivered. You have got to see this thing in the Holy Ghost. Your enemy is after the "Results" of your ministry. There are preachers that tell you all the time: "I'm with you. Yeah, they are with you all right. They're with you to get from your ministry what they can to boost their ministry.

They are so paralyzed at the brain that they don't see it's the Anointing that's working in your ministry, and not you. The defeated one may hinder to a degree the move of God, but he surely can not stop it. There are fault-finder demons on assignment masquerading as discernment. If we are not Acutely aware and focused, this spirit will have us (strong Christians), forming negative opinions and attitudes toward our brother or sister in Christ. When you find yourself thinking ill thoughts and having negative opinions about others, be sure "that" person is under demonic attack. And, the devil is using you to help him destroy that person.

Stay focused, because if you don't, you will never get your stuff back! You are dealing with a relentless foe that is focused. his focus is to destroy at every level and in every direction.

You make sure that you are not being used to help carry out his plans. Make sure you are not a crusader for the devil. Make sure you are not being manipulated by your Bishop, your Pastor, and anyone else. For quite a few of them will try to work the spirit of Jezebel on you if you let them. You see, titles and positions don't move me.

You've got to come right with me or get out of my face and stay out.

We may discover some hidden or on-going sin of a Bishop or Pastor, but what we do with this knowledge shows the measure of our maturity. Yes, regardless of how juicy it could be, it's all in how you handle the information that you have. Look at Jesus. When He looked upon man and saw his sins and iniquities; what did he do? He emptied Himself. He humbled Himself by dying on the cross for our sins. We too, when we find out information on our brother or our sister, we are to not be used of the accuser, but we are to empty ourselves by giving the situation to Jesus-holding that person up in prayer. Jesus didn't judge us, He died for us. (Phil. 2:7-8), *" But made Himself of no reputation, and took upon Him the form of a servant, and was made in the likeness of men: And being found in fashion as a man, He humbled Himself and became obedient unto death, even the death of the cross."*

No one is exempt of being used by the accuser. Someone can come to you with gossip that you start to believe. Please don't start accusing and critizing the person talked about before you've had the chance to get the "truth." If you judge before you know the facts, then you become their judge and help carry out satan's plans to destroy that person. If the devil can use you to discredit the minister (the messenger), he can then discredit his "message."

If you watch this spirit (faultfinding), you'll find it appears on the scene just before or right after an awesome breakthrough. The thing is, satan's plans are to stop the Church of Jesus Christ or a particular Ministry from going forward and stepping into it's destiny. This faultfinding spirit is contagious and it spreads like wildfire. When this spirit infiltrates a person's mind, the accusations that comes with faultfinding, comes with such venom, that a person that knows better, will find themselves seduced by it's influence. satan wants us to take our focus off of Jesus, and focus on issues. And it's the devil that births the issues. But the Apostle Paul tells us to keep our eyes on the Prize, Christ Jesus. Jesus is the Light of the World. To focus on anything else, is to focus on darkness.

We must realize or should I say, "Remember." When we come against our brother/sister, we are then no longer united with them. We are then no longer "one" with them. Jesus' prayer in St. John 17, is that we become one even as He and the Father are One. Let's go there, (St. John 17:20-21), " *Neither pray I for these alone, but for them also which shall believe on me through their word; that they all may be one; as Thou Father art in Me and I in Thee, that they also may be one in Us.: that the world may believe that Thou has sent Me."* So you see, we are to be of one mind. When we are all of one mind, (on one accord), the devil will have to give it up. he'll have to give you back all your stuff, your great-grandparents' stuff, your grandparents' stuff, and your own stuff. Oh yes, if you live Holy, you have authority to speak the word and the devil must give it up!!!!!

Friends that you trusted for years, suddenly appears distant. Yes, the accuser has gotten to them. Long established relationships, strong and foundational, are suddenly shaken. All because of whispers from the accuser of the brethren. Stay Focused!!!!!

When we find someone in a fault, we are to restore them, not destroy them with our tongue. In most cases, the person that's being pounced on, don't even know they're being accused. By the time they hear it, their name and ministry has been slandered. In some cases, the gossip is true. So what if it is. Go to that brother/sister and talk to them, if they're Godly sorry, restore them. Do all you can to see that they get counseling in that area. Don't help the devil destroy them. Even Jesus gave Jezebel space to repent! And just who are you that you are so Holy and in the position to put God's people down? (*Rev. 2:20-21*), " *Notwithstanding, (nevertheless), I have a few things against thee, because thou sufferest that woman Jezebel, which calleth herself a prophetess, to teach and to seduce my servants to commit fornication, and to eat things sacrificed to idols. And I gave her space to repent of her fornication, and she repented not.*

The reason I'm sharing this with you is that all too often, we wonder what is holding up our stuff. I can hear some of yall saying right now, " well, I done prayed, I pay my tithes and offerings, I done seeded into someone else's ministry. Sometimes, we feel if we do all of these things and some more, we will receive God's abundance. Well all of the above are just a few qualifiers. As we get into the Word of God, we will see what hinders us. And just being sensitive to the voice of the Holy Spirit, especially when we know we are moving contrary to the Word of God, just listening and obeying Him when He tells us about ourselves, should bring us back in line with God's Word.

The enemy comes with weapons. he is not an empty handed visitor. You know how it is when you go visiting, you never go empty handed (or at least you shouldn't), especially when you've been invited to dinner. Likewise, the enemy never comes empty handed. he comes with weapons to stake "Your" claim. Most of his weapons, "we" give to him. "Right!" Yes, "Right" we give him weapons to come against ourselves. Most of the time, he doesn't have to create weapons because the Christians that are not focused Jesus, will give him all the weapons he needs to come against their house or their Ministry.

One of these weapons is a lack of knowledge of God. Again, Hosea 4:6.

Well, the accuser of the brethren is just one of the

things that stop you from receiving. Remember, the devil has five thousand plus years experience on us. he feeds upon sin and ignorance. So you see, it's critical that we get knowledge. When we're in ignorance, this leaves room for strongholds (demon spirits). These spirits will rob you of power and joy. Some folks seem to feel that just because they're saved, sanctified, and filled as they say, with the Holy Spirit, they feel they can not be deceived. This is tragic and self deception. Christians are also deceived when they believe that they can not have a demon. Hear me please! Where ever there is darkness, satan rules. I grant you he can not reside in our spirit because that's where the Holy Spirit is. But there are unregenerated minds (the soulish realm). If there's darkness in the soul, he has a legal right to live in darkness.

Also, he lives in a mind (soul) that has not totally surrendered to Jesus. he lives very comfortable there. he also lives very comfortable and laid back in an unrepented mind. Oh, he's at home there, even cooking, eating, and resting.

You see, when we are in error, the Holy Spirit will "Right Away" prompt us to repent, because He knows that this is an area that satan will "Jump on" without hesitation. The Holy Spirit knows too that God wont move in unrepentance. So, the Christian is vulnerable to the enemy. But, we disarm the defeated one when we confess and repent of our sins. The Word of God tells us that when we confess and repent of our sins, that Jesus is just to forgive us of our sins and "cleanse" us from all

Unrighteousness.

Hey my brother, my sister, it's critical that we be focused. The Holy Spirit of God is forever speaking and in order for us to hear what He's saying, we must be discerning at "all" times. I was in the pulpit at this church. And certain ones came up to greet me. And while I was talking to them, I noticed in the background someone else was standing there waiting to talk to me. I felt a prompting from the Holy Spirit that something was not just right coming from the "other" person, but somehow, I missed it. Until the person shook my hand and I knew then what the Holy Spirit was trying to tell me. That person in the back ground shook my hand, and there was an awful heaviness, but it was evil. I missed what the Holy Spirit was showing me. I was so caught up in what the first person was saying, that I was not in tuned with the Holy Spirit and the devil made his move. So you see beloved, we must be focused.

As I was in prayer one morning, the Holy Spirit flashed a co-worker's face before me and asked that I pray for her. It was someone I worked with that had been stabbing me in my back. Well, I loved her but I didn't like her. Did not feel like praying for her, but nevertheless, God said pray for her. So I automatically begin to pray for her protection. (We know not what to pray for as we ought). Not knowing what was going to happen later in the day. Well when I got to work, I told her that the Holy Spirit had me to pray for her protection that morning. She shrugged it off in front of everybody. Well, she went to lunch at noon and about 12:30, she came running back into the office and directly to me. She said to me: Janie, I know why you had to pray for me this morning. She said, I was walking down Market street and all of a sudden a window came from no where. If I had taken another step, I would be dead. But it couldn't happen because you already prayed for me.

This is why we must be focused in the Holy Ghost. It was critical that I obeyed Him in praying for her protection. My God!!!!!! There is no time for playing games, lives are at stake.

Guard your tongue, guard your mind

Keep in mind, Jesus said, "You shall have what you say." Yes, the tongue is powerful. Not only in prayer, but in our everyday talking. We can't talk loosely. That's why it's important that we speak positive over our loved ones daily. Mainly because we don't know what other "words" have been spoken (placed) in the atmosphere. Words are "spirit." The power of life and death is in the power of the tongue. Also, we will be judged by every "idol" word spoken. (Mt. 12:36-37), " *But I say unto you, that every idol word that men shall speak they shall give account thereof in the day of judgement. For by thy words thou shalt be justified, and by thy words, thou shalt be condemned.*" (Mt. 12:34-b) "*for out of the abundance of the heart, the mouth speaketh.*" James told us how powerful the tongue is: (James 3:6) *And the tongue is a fire, a world of iniquity (wickedness or twisted), so is the tongue among our members, that it defileth the whole body, and setteth on fire the course of nature; and it is set on fire of hell.*"

It's so much in God's Word that tells us how we will

not get our stuff back from the devil, yet there is a lot that teaches us how to take back our stuff. God's Word is so pregnant. God looks at what "we say" and then He acts on our words. Whether our words are spoken in prayer or everyday talking, He acts on what He hears. Guess what, the devil does too. So, be aware of your words, you may have to eat them. Remember when Isaiah saw the Lord, his guilt was due to his words. He said, *"woe is me, for I am undone; because I am a man of unclean lips for my eyes have seen the King, the Lord of Hosts.*

Please be aware of criticism of others, because it's really satan accusing the Child of God before our God.

Yes, guard your tongue because that same tongue can either justify you or condemn you. Fill your heart with the Word of God. Where there is abundance (much) in the heart, the mouth will speak. (Mt. 12:34-b) *"...for out of the abundance of the heart, the mouth will speak."* So no matter how negative the situation or circumstance is, speak "Life" to it.

Not too long ago, I was sitting in a church service, and the preacher was preaching a very negative sermon. He kept telling the people that they were going to die, and that everybody was going to die sooner or later. Well, the Holy Spirit bought it back to my memory, (1 Cor. 15:51-52), " *Behold, I show you a mystery; we shall not all sleep, but we shall be changed, in a moment, in the twinkling of an eye, at the last trump: for the trumpet shall sound, and the dead shall be raised incorruptible, and we shall be changed."* So, we are not all going to die naturally, because the Word of God says so. But it troubled me that the preacher would allow those words to flow. And of course, the people cried out, "Amen." it's sooo much that is agreed upon that we better be mindful what we're saying "Amen" to.

We must be positive because of the power that is in the tongue. Remember, life and death is in the power of the tongue. We're in warfare, and we must look at how, throughout Scripture, Jesus talked, and mimic Him. Say what Jesus says. There must be balance in our lives. This is why it's so important that we get Scripture relative to situations and circumstances in our lives, and pray the Word of God over these problems. Use your tongue, Work it! It's a weapon that fights for you. As long as you have God's Word on your tongue, you have a mighty weapon, and you are a mighty warrior. You see, we don't even fight like the world fight. The world go into battle with guns. We go into battle with "the Sword." (The Word of God) And it's greater than any natural or spiritual weapon. Jesus is that Two-edged Sword. Yes, this Sword have two cutting edges. It cuts going and it cuts coming. Well, some of our tongues do that same thing in negative ways, and these things ought not to be.

Instead of using our tongues to tear down "people," we need to use our tongues to tear down the kingdom of hell. That's our real enemy. In fact, that's where the real battle is. So, let's be mindful of all we say. I even try to monitor my thoughts. And I noticed, if my thoughts are pure and positive, I'll speak such. But if my thoughts are evil and negative, I'll speak that too. So I try to be mindful of my thoughts and bring them captive from time to time. We must bring our thoughts under subjection to the Holy Spirit. This is why it's important to be filled with the Holy Spirit. If we're filled with the Spirit, we will train our hearts and minds to think Jesus thoughts. We'll teach ourselves how to bring our thoughts captive to the things of God. We'll fill our hearts with spiritual things (Holy), so that what's in the heart will come out of the mouth. Again, (Mt. 12:34-b), " *Out of the abundance of the heart, the mouth speaketh."*

So, use that tongue to cut up the devil's plans. Guard your tongue, guard your mind. That's the problem these days, the mind of man is allowed to just go berserk. Thinking all kinds of thoughts, saying what's on the mind without checking what's happening.

Check yourself!!! You can not allow your mind to wander. If you do, your tongue can not be controlled. You will speak your whole heart. (Prov. 29:11), "A *fool uttereth all his heart; but a wise man keepeth it in till afterwards. Guard your mind,* (Rom. 7:23), " *But I see another law in my members, warring against the law of my mind, and bringing me into captivity to the law of sin which is in my members.* Again, guard your mind with all diligence. Because your mind is where warfare begins. It's where the devil do battle. It where he bring fears - in the mind. Guard the mind at all cost. Don't allow your eyes to see just anything. Even be careful watching television especially, because in watching television, believe it or not, you are depositing stuff not only in your spirit, but also in your mind. Don't allow just any and everything to come out of your mouth. That's why it's very important to be focused in your thoughts, because your thoughts will flow out of your mouth.

When you speak, speak words of encouragement, words of wisdom. Speak words of deliverance. Somebody need a Word from the Lord. Will they hear it coming from your mouth??? Guard your tongue, guard your mind.

CHAPTER 3

DISARM THE DEVIL

(I Cor. 10:4-5), " For the weapons of our warfare are not carnal, but mighty through God to the pulling down of strongholds. Casting down imaginations and every high thing that exhalteth itself against the knowledge of God, and bringing into captivity every thought to the obedience of Christ:"

We are to pull down strongholds. What are strongholds? Well, I'm glad you asked, smile. This is a spiritual fortress whereby satan and his demons hide. And, likely so. How fitting it is for cowards to hide! These fortresses exist only in the mind. In order to attain victory in any area, we must access what the stronghold is and then commence to tear it down.

Stronghold: a fortified dwelling. We're going to expose some strongholds so you will know how to pray and pull them down. If there is to be deliverance, we must first pull down the house that house the defeated one. I'm going to share some information on strongholds with you:

Now, there are different types of strongholds. We have a stronghold in Jesus. For He is our protection. He is our defense. But as you know, I am talking about satans's strongholds. Our thinking can be a stronghold. If we exalt ourselves above the knowledge of God, we give the defeated one a place of influence. Jesus said that we are not to give foot-hold to the devil.

The devil can not possess you as a Christian, but if there's darkness in you, he can live in that darkness and oppress you. Therefore, please be aware, a Christian can have a devil, but if he/she is a true Child of God, the devil can not live in their spirit. The spirit of the Christian houses the Holy Ghost; however, if there is an area of unrepentance (darkness), the defeated one lives in darkness.

Fear

Fear is another stronghold. Fear is the devil's kind of faith. Fear taunts you, and it's time you be free of it. Fear is bondage. It paralyzes your tongue and your brain. You can't talk when you fear because you can't think clearly. When you're in fear, you regress or you mark time. You will go absolutely no where. This is why it's important we renew our minds. When you have Jesus, there really should not be fear. He has set us free from this demonic stronghold. (I John 4:18), *"There is no fear in Love. Perfect Love cast out fear because fear has torment. He that feareth is not made perfect in love."* Keep in mind, once we know what is in the Name of Jesus, the marriage is consummated. In other words, we are to put on Jesus. We are to have the very nature of Jesus. We are to walk in His character. His character is the Nine Fruit of the Spirit. Everybody is running after the Nine Gifts, but the Anointing have a problem with the gifts until we walk in the fruit. Our lives must be thoroughly preoccupied with Jesus, the Son of the Living God.

You can be saved, sanctified, and filled with the Holy Spirit, yet living in torment because of fear. Yes, you are saved, sanctified, and filled with the Holy Spirit, but some of yall need deliverance! And you need it NOW! Fear has torment and must be exposed for what it is and you must bind that spirit and cast it out.

There is a stronghold of self-deception. Don't think the devil wont go there! he will stop at nothing to cause you to deceive yourself. And it's hard to talk to people that are self-deceived, and especially Christians. When you're deceived, you don't know you're deceived, "because" you are deceived. Any area of our heart or mind that is not totally surrendered to Jesus, is a door opened for satanic attack.

There is a "new-born" Christian I know. He knows all things. And because he knows all things he is a Prime Target for satanic attack. We were discussing God's Word one day and he sort of got off in left field. He was talking so "off the wall" about God and His Word, I asked, "Where are you coming from?" He says, "The Word of God." I asked him to show me where that Scripture was.

He says, "It's in the 'Lost Books' of the Bible." So I told him to never quote those books, because during Canonization of the Holy Scriptures, God, the Holy Ghost, did not allow those books for His own reasons. " Why should we reach back for "word" that was not allowed in the Holy Scriptures by the Holy Ghost? I asked him to please do not quote, believe, or use any part of Scripture that the Holy Spirit did not allow to be placed in the Bible. He still felt that he was not in error or deceived. satan loves it when Christians are deceived. he throws a party and celebrates because he knows that he can easily manipulate that Christian that is self-deceived.

This young man, when he was in the world, he was a manipulator, (witchcraft), so when he came into the Kingdom of God, he felt he could still manipulate God's people, not knowing that there are the three Revelation Gifts, (Word of Wisdom, Word of Knowledge, and Discernment). But then, when you are operating in familiar spirits, you are deceived!!! I don't know how I got off on that, but to God be the Glory!

Whenever there's a habit of sin, the devil is robbing the believer of Joy, Power, and Peace. And this is part of our Covenant Right under the Abrahamic Covenant. I want all that is promised to me under that Covenant. Believe it or not, if you are being robbed of your joy, power, and peace, the devil has positioned a stronghold there! Because where there is no joy, there's sadness. Where there is no power, the devil rules. Where there is no peace, there's confusion and chaos. The Word of God declare, the Joy of the Lord is your strength. If your joy is taken, you then become a weakling. God has given us power over the defeated one (*Luke* 10:19). Your foe will tear you to shreds if you have no power. And the defeated one knows whether you have power with God or not. Remember when the seven sons of sceva tried to cast devils out? The devils rose up and said to sceva's sons, "Jesus I know, Paul I know, but who are you. In other words you are not going to do nothing with me because you have no power. And you know what happened to sceva's sons. Don't lose your peace.

The Word of God declares that Jesus is our Peace. He is the Prince of Peace.

There are so many ways we can disarm the enemy. But, number one is Repentance. We can pray and anoint with oil and everything else, but if there's no repentance, there will be absolutely no deliverance.

I'm sharing all of this with you so you can know how to pray in order to disarm the devil. strongholds don't just appear overnight. The devil plants seeds and waits for growth (reaction). When you react in his favor, he knows he have your mind. When he sees germination, (sprouts of development of that seed), he waits for maturity. Hidden sins, you know those Secret sins, the enemy will use those to tare you asunder.

That's why there is so much power in Repentance. It's called "Exposure." When you expose yourself, there is nothing else left for the devil to black- mail you with, HAHAHA!!!!! But if you have hidden "secret sins" God forbid, you better get it out in the open so you can be delivered. You don't have to go to no one but God and confess your sins too. Don't just go to Him and ask forgiveness for your many sins. You know how we can be sometimes. Tell God "ALL" about it. If you lied, fornicated, committed adultery, etc. just say, "God in the name of Jesus, I told a lie and tell Him about that lie. Tell him, " I fornicated." Just "say" the sin. Hey, try it, you'll get free, I guarantee you. But, go to Him with a Repentant heart.

Your life is at stake. The Holy Ghost will enable you to repent and come back to God-fresh, whole, and ready to begin again, and this time, in true Holiness. Where there's repentance, strongholds must fall. But once you are delivered, there will be pressures from the evil one. There will also be pressure from your flesh for you to fall back. And you may be tempted to surrender a small portion of your life, well this is what strongholds are made of. This is the foundation of a stronghold. No, when we come to Christ, or when we come back to Christ, we must surrender "ALL" to Jesus. Give the devil no room for black-mail.

After you're delivered, keep in mind: (Mt. 12:43-45), "*When the unclean spirit is gone out of a man, he walketh through dry places seeking rest, and findeth none. Then he saith, I will return into my house from whence I came; and when he is come, he findeth it empty, swept, and garnished. Then goeth he and taketh himself seven other spirits more wicked (twisted) than himself, and they enter in and dwell there: and the last state of that man is worse than the first." Even so shall it be also unto this wicked generation.*" Jesus is warning us of what can happen "after" we're delivered. And do not deceive yourself, the enemy of your soul is real. But he's spirit, and we can fight him with our spiritual weapons. That's why it's so important to build an arsenal of spiritual weapons.

Because you can not fight that which is spirit with natural weapons. Oh, but when we "prepare" ourselves and fight in the Spirit, we are an awesome army! We fight spirit with spirit!!!

(*Eph.* 6:12), *"For we wrestle not against flesh and blood, but against principalities, against powers, against the rulers of the darkness of this world, against spiritual wickedness in high places."* I want to break this

Scripture down and share this with you: When we wrestle, it's hard. You're putting strength against strength. **principalities:** are territories that are ruled by a prince. And a prince is a ruler that ranks just below it's king's powers. he holds a high position. But no matter how high they are, they all come subject to Jesus Christ.

They can't even separate us from His love. (*Rom.* 8:38-39), *"For I am persuaded, that neither death nor life, nor angels, nor principalities, nor powers, nor things present, nor things to come, nor height, nor depth, nor any other creature, shall be able to separate us from the love of God which is in Christ Jesus, our Lord."* **powers:** are forces, they influence, they produce effect. They have authority over other evil spirits to influence them. **rulers:** they are governors in the spirit realm. They have an itinerary and they rule according to their itinerary, the **dark forces** of this world. **wicked spirits:** that word, "wicked" is a derivative of wicker as in wicker furniture, meaning "Twisted." These are even more twisted than some spirits. These spirits are morally evil. They show great skill in their wicked twisted little minds.

This let us know that the devil has well thought out plans. he has an army and it is well regimented. Yes, he has it very well organized. If anything is out of order (satan's order) he will strictly discipline these devils. Your enemy is a strategist, and he has sprayed a spirit of lathery over the Body of Christ, and some of us are sleeping, wide awake, but yet sleeping. Unaware, sleep-walking, blind to the strategies of the defeated one. This is why Jesus said,

(I Thess. 5:6-8), " *Therefore, let us not sleep as do others; but let us watch and be sober. For they that sleep, sleep in the night, and they that be drunken are drunken in the night. But, let us who are of the day be sober, putting on the breast plate of faith and love; and for an helmet, the hope of salvation."* Jesus also spoke of being alert and sober. "Be sober, be vigilant; because your adversary, the devil, as a roaring lion walketh about seeking whom he may devour: See, we've got to know what our enemy is about. Learn his strategies and turn them back on him.

When a stronghold or a strongman is fully armed, he can guard his house. No one can touch his possessions. (satan considers us his possessions). Yet, when someone comes along stronger than he, he can be stripped of his armor, thus he's disarmed. Once he's disarmed, the devil might as well say his prayers, because it's over! You can then go in and take his stuff, or rather your stuff. This is what I'm sharing with you, that is how to go in his territory and take back "all" of your stuff!!!

When Jesus died, He stripped the devil of all his powers. In other words, Jesus disarmed him. So now, tell me please, why should you allow someone that is already defeated to defeat you???? he's already defeated!!!

Just like we're already seated in heavenly places, the devil is already defeated. he's acting like he's "all that," and this is what confuses some of the Body of Christ, because they see actions and reactions of the evil one. I don't care what he's doing or has done, he's defeated! Listen up, come a little closer, he's defeated!!!! I don't care what he dangles in my face, he's defeated!, he's defeated!, he's defeated!!! The Blood of Jesus defeated him!! he's defeated! My sister, my brother, you better "See This." You better come out of your religious stupor and open your eyes. It's critical that you know he's defeated! Only when you truly know he's defeated, will you go get your stuff!

I used to play baseball when I was a kid. I loved the game. We were playing baseball one day. I was the pitcher and the kid at bat hit a home-run. The problem was, she hit the ball in our neighbor's back yard. My neighbor had a big bad bull dog. The neighbor hollered out the window that it was O.K. to go get the ball, and that the dog was tied. Well, knowing how bad that dog was, I didn't believe her.

She came out and got our ball. The dog came out of his doghouse and I saw that he "was" tied with a "strong" link chain and could not go where the ball was. Someone hit the ball in her yard again. She said it's o.K.

to go get it. Well, I was confident this time because I knew that the dog was secured and couldn't come where the ball was. I was confident in what I knew. So, I went in the yard and got my ball. The dog barked loud and hard, but I knew he couldn't touch me. The same thing is true about our stuff. Jesus has a chain around satan's neck. he can't go but so far. But you've got to know this and you've got to be confident in what you know. "GO GET YOUR STUFF!!!!!"

Command the devil to put it back. On yes, you got authority and power to make him put it back. Put back your marriage. Put back your job. Put back your promotion. Put back your home. Put back your new house. Put back your new car. Put it all back. You are anointed of God. Exercise your anointing. The Anointing is what will bring your stuff back to you. The defeated understands the anointing. Remember he "once" was lucifer the anointed cherub. It's over! Done with! Zip!!!! Let him know that you "know" who you are. Verbiage itself does not move him, but when he hears verbiage with knowledge of the Name of Jesus and knowledge of what's in that Name, this is what backs him down. Oh, I know what I'm talking about. Again, look at the seven sons of sceva in (Acts 19: 14), *"and there was seven sons of one sceva, a jew and chief of the priest which did so. And the evil spirit answered and said, ' Jesus I know and Paul I know; but who are you; and the man in whom the evil spirit was leaped on them and overcame them and prevailed against them so that they fled out of that house naked and wounded.* This is obvious the devil knows who has power over him.

We must go in the enemy's camp and take over!

I'm tired of seeing God's people live in defeat! I'm tired of seeing God's people live in poverty. I'm tired of seeing God's people experience sickness and disease. We are Abraham's seed! When is this going to hit home with the Body! God made a Covenant with Abraham. And if we are Abraham's seed (and we are), then that "Same" Covenant trickles right on down to us. (*Gen.* 17:7-), " *And I will establish my Covenant between me and thee, and thy seed after thee in their generations for an everlasting Covenant, to be a God unto thee and to thy seed after thee. And I will give unto thee, and to thy seed after thee, the land wherein thou art a stranger. All the land of Canaan for an everlasting possession; I will be their God."*

Yes, yes, yes, what God has for Abraham belongs to us. We are his seed after him. Do you see it? Oh, you've got to Work this!

Oh yes, I'm not quite done with the issue of secret sins. It's vitally important to guard against secret sins. Maintain a continual alert against this stronghold. They are destroyers. We must protect our character. Sometimes we do things that are completely out of our character, but often times, that have a lot to do with who we associate with. So many of our great leaders have fallen because of secret sins. Secret unrepented sins must be dealt with and right away. David cried several times in the Word of God, "How are the mighty fallen!" David's mourning for Jonathan and Saul, he cried out three times. (II *Sam.* 1:17-27). David described the beginning of their ministries as beautiful in *verse*19, mighty lovely, and pleasant. Swifter than eagles, *verse* 23, stronger than lions. *Verse* 24, able to clothe others in scarlet, able to put ornaments of God on others.

Many ministries started out this way. Many were mighty and strong in the Lord. But, something happened along the way. They held on to secret sins.

They didn't repent of these sins, so the defeated one black-mailed them. So, you see how the Mighty can fall. Not only is God watching and listening, so is your enemy. And, if you don't let God reveal certain sins to you for your repentance, satan will reveal these sins to others. This is how ministries are destroyed. When the Holy Spirit starts to convict us of these sins, we should be sensitive to Him and obey.

Stop Hypocritting

Another way we disarm the defeated one is to stop Hypocritting. Most religious hypocrites wants to show-boat (be seen and heard). They want others to think highly of them. In fact, most hypocrites are **uneducated AND unteachable**. When you're educated, most people that are, have a strong sense of who they are. It's the Dum Dumms, (sorry) that need validation as to who they are. What they do is measure themselves by the standards of others. They're confused, so to get the spotlight off of them in a negative way, they pretend to be someone they're not. Thus they hypocrite. This is somewhat of a checklist to determine who hypocrites are.

1. They are great actors
2. Everything they do is to be seen and heard of men
3. They want others to think they've got inside information on God.
4. Instead of releasing God's people to freedom, hypocrites put you in bondage
5. Hypocrites causes God's people to fear
6. Hypocrites have the "Form" of God, but denies His Power

Hypocrites don't care about freeing God's people up in the Holy Ghost. They would rather exalt "Form" over Substance. You will find hypocrites to be very traditional and "stiff." Things must go their way or no way. They're caught up in rules and regulations and presuppositions that determines how and who God moves through. A hypocrite is a pathetic being that is caught up in their own thing. (Mt. 23:23-27), *"Scribes and Pharisees, and hypocrites! for ye pay tithes of mint and anise, and cummin and have omitted the weightier matters of the law, judgement, mercy, and faith; these ought ye to have done, and not to leave the other undone. Ye blind guides which strain at a gnat and swallow a camel. Woe unto you scribes and Pharisees and hypocrites. For ye make clean the outside of the cup, and of the platter, but within, they are full of extortion and excess. Thou blind Pharisee, cleanse first that which is within the cup and platter, that the outside of them may be clean also. Woe unto you scribes and Pharisees and hypocrites! For ye are like unto whited sepulchers, which indeed appear beautiful outward, but are within full of dead men's bones of all uncleanness."*

We should search our hearts to see if we are hypocrites. If we are hypocritting, we can't take our stuff back until we get it right. Only when our lives line up with the Word of God, are we in the position to go in the enemy's camp and take over.

Stop trying to give what you don't have

Still hypocriting huh? Why not go get what you don't have and walk in it, instead of fronting? I say this because I know of a particular pastor that is clearly not walking in the Pastorate. The people of God that sits under this pastor are perishing and they are literally and spiritually drying up. In my opinion, God's call to pastor is not on this person's life. Maybe God's call to preach, but not to pastor. (Jer. 3:15), " *And I will give you pastors according to mine own heart which shall feed you with knowledge and understanding."*

There is no revelation knowledge coming from this pastor. I really don't have too much sympathy for this person. I sympathize with the sheep that sits under this shepherd, because they're learning absolutely nothing. This pastor's children were all members of other churches and they all came back to help the family church out. It's not the family's job. The family were not called to pastor.

This leader is hypocritting. In place of the Rhema Word of God preached and taught, they're caught up in singing and constantly screaming during sermons. I know it may to some of you sound as though it's O.K. to do this.

And I agree. It is O.K. to do this if you are teaching something to God's people. The singing and the screaming, all of this will not replace the Word of God. There is much teaching and deliverance needed there. I hurt for the people for they are the ones suffering. Pastors of this kind are hypocritting. They replace teaching the people of God with things that are not good for them. It appears that the defeated one has come in and sprayed a spirit of larthargy over the congregation, and they're sound asleep. Therefore, when they're manipulated (controlled), they're not aware at all that they're being used. God is not pleased with this.

These people play the part, but yet deny God's power. They wear the "Form" quite well, but God has said, I am sick of the form.

(Isaiah 1:11-), " *To what purpose is the multitude of your sacrifice unto me? Saith the Lord. I am full of the burnt offerings of rams and the fat of fed beasts: and I delight not in the blood of bullocks or lambs or of he goats. When you come to appear before me, who hath required this at your hand to tread my courts? Bring no more vain oblations; incense is an abomination unto me; the new moons and sabbaths, the calling of assemblies, I cannot away with; it is iniquity, even the solemn meeting. Your new moons and your appointed feasts, my soul hateth. They are trouble unto me. I am weary to bear them. And when ye spread forth your hands, I will hide mine eyes from you: Yea, when ye make many prayers, I will not hear. Your hands are full of blood. Wash you, make you clean, put away the evil of your doings from before mine eyes; cease to do evil; learn to do well, seek judgement; relieve the oppress, judge the fatherless, pleased for the widow. Come now, let us reason together,* saith the Lord: though your sins be as scarlet they shall be white as snow. Though they be red like crimson, they shall be as wool."

This Holy Word of God is saying much. The finger is being pointed at this particular pastor, but it's really pointed at us all. You see, stuff like this keeps us from getting in position to take our stuff back from the enemy. It also ties the hand of God's people as well. Because, if they are without knowledge, they will be destroyed by the enemy.

(Jer. 23:1-2), *"Woe unto the pastors that destroy and scatter the sheep of my pasture! saith the Lord. Therefore, thus saith the Lord God of Israel, against the pastors that feed my people;"*

(Jer.10:21), *" For the pastors are become brutal, and have not sought the Lord: therefore they shall not prosper and all their flocks shall be scattered."*

(Jer. 12:10-11), *" Many pastors have destroyed my vineyards, they have trodden my portion under foot. They have made my pleasant portion a desolate wilderness. They have made it desolate, and being desolate, it mourneth unto me; the whole land is made desolate, because no man layeth it to heart."*

(Jer. 23:22), *" But if they had stood in my counsel, and had caused my people to hear my words, then they should have turned them from their evil way; and from the evil of their doings.Ye have scattered my flock and driven them away, and have not visited them; behold, I will visit upon you the evil of your doings, saith the Lord."*

In order to teach God's people His Word, His Word must first dwell in us richly. If not, how can we give what we don't have? Time is out for Fronting. Fronting is old and dead. If we're called to the Five-Fold Ministry, then we are the Administrative gifts to the "Body." And, we can not administer the Word of God unless the Word of God is in us richly. Whatever you do, administrative team, do not manipulate God's people. Rather, feed them, love them, nurture them, embrace them and deposit the Word of God in them. How else can they hear if a Preacher don't preach to them, if a Teacher don't teach them, if a Prophet don't direct them, if an Apostle don't find a place for them, if a Pastor don't nurture them. How else can they learn the Word of God if we don't put it out there? If we are hypocrites, the people of God doomed and they become prey in the hand of the enemy.

Again, (Rom. 10:14-15). *" How then shall they call on Him in whom they have not believed? And how shall they believe in Him of whom they have not heard? And how shall they hear without a preacher? And how shall they preach except they be sent? As it is written, how beautiful are the feet of them that preach the gospel of peace and bring glad tidings of good things! But they have not all obeyed the gospel, for Esaias saith Lord, who hath believed our report? So then faith cometh by hearing, and hearing by the Word of God.*

CHAPTER 4

FROM FOOTHOLD TO STRONGHOLD

Our Arch enemy is shrewd and he hates us with a passion that's almost indescribable. This is why it is critical that we walk in this Commandment. (Luke 10:27-28), " And *he answering said, "Thou shalt love the Lord thy God with all thy heart, and with all thy soul, and with all thy strength, and with all thy mind; and thy neighbor as thyself."* If we walk in this love, you can be sure that God's got our back.

Foothold: A secure position; a secure place for a foot.
Stronghold: A place having strong defenses; fortress.
Fortress: A fortified place
Fortified: A defended, guarded, safeguarded, protected, manned, barricaded, armed, strong, covered, surrounded, hidden, camouflaged.

Wow!!! These definitions are an eye opener. They are a mind opener too! My brother, my sister, we're in warfare and this devil mean business. This devil is destroying in every direction and the Church is sleeping, and when the Church is finally awake, they're frying chicken!

If we're sleeping, please tell me, how in the name of God can we go to the enemy's camp and get our stuff? Do we go yawning, not focused? Do we go dreaming our stuff back? No! Some try to, but the Bible says that nothing comes to a sleeper but a dream. Not your stuff, a dream! This is pathetic! The "Body" is sound asleep. You know how the defeated one created a stronghold? he starts with a foothold. And as you just read, a foothold is a secured place for "a foot." There are some footholds planned for our lives daily. The enemy has built strongholds in our family line generations ago.

But it all begins with a foothold that was ignored by a family member or family members.

Or somebody compromised and the foothold was allowed to take root and develop into a stronghold. Drug addicts usually start out using only a small amount of drugs and they usually stick with "that" one particular drug. But over a period of time, they need more and more of various kinds of drugs to satisfy that craving that has now possessed them. I'm sure at first, it all begins with having a little fun. Harmless, innocent fun, so the person thought. I'm sure addiction didn't even cross their mind. But now, behold, the "drug addict." Hey, you can not play with satan. You can not play with sin. However innocent the sin "appears" to be, the truth of the matter is, sin is "deadly." You see, satan is "REAL SERIOUS: about your destruction.

This sort of remind me when I was in management training class years ago. I was taught to keep a running manual on each employee year after year. Keep this manual on positive things they do and especially on the negative. In doing this, I learn to track habits, positive and negative. I got so good at doing this that I could just about predict each one's actions or reactions during a given situation. Well, the defeated one has been doing this same thing every since he's been in the earth. This is why he's called the familiar spirit. he's familiar with us. And a lot of us go tip-toeing through the tulips daily and not focused. he thrives on our ignorance. he loves this mentality because he can do just what he wants to, when he wants to, and how he wants to. In this case, he can set up a stronghold in the life and family line of the person that is not focused, without even starting at a foothold. he's cunning, but with some of yall, he doesn't have to be cunning.

Because you're not watching, he can and will play right in front of your face and you wont even see him, because you are asleep! I noticed that the defeated one believes in long-term planning. Yes, he'll wait you out. Have you heard the old saying, " a journey of a thousand miles begins with a single step?" That's what your enemy is looking at, that thousand miles. he doesn't mind slow-walking you down. We've got to be focused, not on the devil, but on what's happening around us.

Sin is dangerous. When you dabble in sin, you expose your soul to appetites that will pull you deeper and deeper into the clutches of satan until you find yourself right in the middle of a stronghold. Stay focused, guard your mind. The evil one will try to plant images in your mind that will eventually snare you. his desire is to plant strongholds in your life. he will use anything and anybody to snare you and keep you snared! But there come a time when "you" must put out all the stops. You must get fed up with making do. You must get fed up with divorce. You must get fed up with constant anger in the marriage. You must get fed up with your sons and daughters on drugs. You must get fed up with having your home and car repossessed. You must get fed up with having little money, some money, but never enough. You must get tired of having to file bankruptcy. You must get tired of all the females in your family having babies out of wedlock. You must get tired of family sickness and diseases coming down through the family lineage. You must get fed up and say TIME OUT!!! And not only say it, but DO something about it!

Tell the defeated one, it's over! Hold-up! he is defeated isn't he! So, why in the name of God, why would you let someone that is "already defeated" defeat you? Please answer this one! Sometime we need to be jolted back to reality.

Strongholds of occultism

So you're Saved now. You're Sanctified and Filled with the Blessed Holy Ghost. You came out of that occult and now walking Holy for God, and everybody is fine. "WRONG" (*Leviticus* 19:26-*b*), " This is telling us not to practice divination or sorcery, (witchcraft). (*Deut.* 7:25-

26), "The graven images of their gods shall ye burn with fire: thou shalt not desire the silver or gold that is on them, nor take it unto thee, lest thou be snared therein, for it is an abomination to the Lord thy God. Neither shalt thou bring an abomination into thine house lest thou be a cursed thing like it, but thou shalt utterly detest it; and thou shalt utterly abhor it; for it is a cursed thing.

The occult is forever in our faces. You'll find it in games. (dungeons and dragons, ouija boards, channeling, horoscopes, and many other forms of witchcraft and even satan worship). Sometimes folks think they are home free when they receive Christ, and this is true to a degree. When you've walked away from occultism and received Jesus as your Savior and Lord, that was the first step. You have to go back and do some erasing so that the defeated one cannot create a trail to follow you in your new found life in Christ Jesus. In other words, some deliverance is needed. Yes, we are hidden in Jesus, but that wall of the occult has to be destroyed. The occult is indeed a stronghold, a fortified place. Just as Jericho was a fortified city. The walls were so strong that houses were built on the walls, and on the roof of the houses were streets where inhabitants of the city raced their chariots on. It was a strong fortified city, yet when Israel obeyed God, the walls of the city fell down. Not only did they fall down, the Bible declares that the walls fell down "flat." (Joshua 6:20), " *So the people shouted when the priests blew with the trumpets: and it came to pass, when the people heard the sound of the trumpets, and the people shouted with a great shout, that the wall fell down flat."*

No matter how Saved you are, if strongholds are still in your life, you need deliverance. You wont be able to go into the enemy's camp and take what's yours until you first destroy the stronghold. That's what the Anointing does. The Anointing destroys the yokes of bondage.

The world is overcome with evil and we need to raise a caution. This evil didn't just start. Yes, it's now a stronghold, but it started with a foothold! Some of yall are tolerating evil. This can be the result of a stronghold, or the beginning of a foothold. Check it out, because either way, you're going to have to stop the enemy, if you're to get your stuff back. We are to show no tolerance for evil. It's getting to be a common practice these days in our churches, to tolerate evil that it. There are folks singing on the choir and sitting in the pulpit and they're shacking up. And the Pastor/Bishop knows it. But, because they pay their tithes, it's tolerated! We can not accept just anything.

We can not embrace evil to keep peace. Sometime issues must be confronted. We can not embrace what the Holy Word of God calls evil. We just can not do it! Folks need to be told "point blank" that they are living in sin. Stop trying to be everybody's friend. Stop trying to keep this kind of peace, tolerating any and everything in order to accomplish false peace. I say "false peace" because that's what it is. Jesus is the only true Peace. He's the Prince of Peace. Some churches are, or should I say Pastors are tolerating homosexuals and lesbians in the pulpit and in the choirs and in other high places in the churches. Bishops/Pastors, these things are abominable to God. These people need to be delivered. What is your problem? Do you hate these people that much that you would rather see them go to hell via the church? You would rather please man and put these people in high places, rather than cast that devil out of them? If you cast the devil out, they can then serve God in the beauty of Holiness.

Yes, I am hard on Bishops/Pastors because I see sooo much! Besides, the call to Pastor is on my life. I'm not walking in it yet and I wont until God releases me to do so. My concern right now are strongholds and pulling them down.

RENEW YOUR MIND

Do you know that even though you are Saved, Sanctified, and filled with the Holy Spirit, your mind must be renewed? (Romans 12:2), " *And be not conformed to this world, but be ye transformed by the renewing of your mind, that ye may prove what is that good, and acceptable, and perfect will of God.*" Once we leave satan and come over on the Lord's side, we've got to re-establish our way of thinking. When we are unsaved, we are in agreement or conformed to the ways of this world's system. But the Holy Ghost, by the mouth of the Apostle Paul said, we are to be transformed, character change, change of condition etc. An un-regenerated mind is a stronghold and must be renewed. When we renew our minds, we re-establish our thinking, we build our character as the character of Christ Jesus. In other words, we are to live the Nine Fruit of the Spirit as it is a perfect depiction of Jesus' character.

We must adopt Jesus' attitudes about all things, that we may prove to ourselves that which is good and acceptable and the perfect will of God. Only with a renewed mind can we really get to know God in His Holiness and Perfection. We can not see Him through the eyes of this world, but when our minds are renewed (this is something we have to do), we see Him through the eyes of the spirit man via the Holy Spirit.

Renew: to make new or fresh; to re-establish: revive; to put in fresh supply, re-awaken, regenerate, rehabilitate, replace, refurbish, redo, overhaul, recover, renovate, bring up to date, make like new, replace.

Yes, there's some stuff in our minds that must be replaced once we come to Christ. Remember, the old man is dead, or should be. After we're Saved, we must work on Deliverance. It's a daily process. As the Apostle Paul says, "we die daily, "in this flesh that is." We've got to put this flesh under subjection/submission to the Holy Spirit. Often times, this flesh hinders us from coming into God's Rest. It also hinders God's Best for our lives. It often keeps us at arm's length from getting our stuff!!!

Now, when we renew our minds, this flesh will have to come subject to the Spirit of God. For if the mind is renewed, (the soul which makes up our thoughts, our intellect, our emotions), it must come subject to the things of God. For the spirit man is already subject to the things of God. The Holy Spirit dwells in our spirit. And He's constantly seeking for our growth, our renewal, renovation, revival, or rehabilitation. Yes, we are to go from Glory to Glory. You will find God is always be a seeker of change for us. He doesn't change for He is God, but He seeks for us to constantly change. Look at His Mercies: the Word of God declares that His Mercies are brand new every morning. This means that you and I are not moving on yesterdays' Mercy, but today's!!!!!

Train your mind to think the thoughts of God. Let this "same" mind be in you that was also in Christ Jesus. (Romans 8:6-8), " *For to be carnally minded is death; but to be spiritually minded is life and peace. Because the carnal mind is enmity (hatred) against God: for it is not subject to the law of God, neither indeed can be.*" So then, they that are in the flesh can not please God. When we renew our minds, it means to do just that. In Eden before sin, our minds were new. We were in innocence until sin came into the world.. So now, we must re-new. Renew means "again," or "as before." We must get our minds back to where it were before sin came into Eden. Again, they were in total innocence. They depended "Solely" on God. Without question, Adam walked with God daily in the cool of the day. And two can not walk together except they be agreed (one mind). Adam was in total obedience (harmony) to the God of Glory.

Keep in mind what I just quoted from the Holy Scriptures: the carnal mind is at odds with the spirit. It hates the mind of the spirit man. This is why it must be subdued. If it's not brought under subjection,/submission, it will produce death. Again, (Romans 8:6), " *To be carnally minded is death, but to be spiritually minded is life and peace.* The carnal mind can not come subject to God, but we can "bring" it captive. Oh yes! We "must" bring it captive!

When we renew our minds, God calls for "Soundness" of mind. When we get to know the mind of Christ, that's when we come into soundness. We're to get knowledge. In fact, knowledge produces soundness of mine. But not the knowledge as that of the Pharisees. You know the Pharisees??? The religious folks. Much head knowledge??? They had much knowledge of the Holy Scriptures, but the Holy Spirit uses the Word of God to fight with. (The Sword of the Spirit is the Word of God). The Pharisees had the Word of God, but they didn't know and didn't care to know the Spirit of the Word of God. So, their knowledge is empty. To have the knowledge of God without the Spirit of that knowledge, will do a lot of damage. This is what destroys marriages. This is what pushes people from God and destroys churches.

The Word of God declares, (Matt. 4:4), " *But he answered and said, It is written, man should not live by bread alone, but by every Word that "Proceedeth" out of the mouth of God*". Now that word, "Proceedeth" is constantly in the present tense. Getting knowledge of God should always be a constant thing. We must get to know the God of His Word!

There are many people I know that can quote Scripture after Scripture. But that's not enough. The Pharisees are alive and well in today's churches. They search the Holy Scriptures throughly. And, Jesus told them, "you search the Scriptures, and in them you think you have eternal life. But the Scriptures speaks of me! I am eternal life!!! (I'm paraphrasing of course) don't be at all anxious about getting to know God's Word without getting to know Him. Soundness of mind is in Christ Jesus. In other words, soundness of mind comes from a relationship with Jesus the Christ of God.

There are many modern day Pharisees. They know God's Word, but don't have the slightest clue about the Holy Spirit. They can quote chapter for chapter (in fact, one of the requirements of that day was to quote the Old Testament word for word), and are quick to argue God's Holy Word. They don't have a clue that the Holy Scriptures are Breathe into by the Holy Spirit. (Spirit Breathe). They will always reach in their back pocket for their doctrine, and we Do Know the deal on their doctrine, don't we??? Renew your Mind.

FOOTHOLDS

Don't allow not one devil to get through to you or your loved ones.

As I shared with you earlier, a foothold is a secured place for a foot. And Jesus said, don't even give foothold (no space), to the devil. (I Peter 5:8),

" *Be sober, be vigilant; because your adversary the devil, as a roaring lion, walketh about, seeking whom he may devour."* That word "devour" means to swallow "whole." In other words, he wants nothing left of you. Jesus has already said, the enemy desires to sift us as wheat. But then Jesus said he can't because "I have prayed for you," or I have interceded for you. Your enemy is so evil and hate you so much that if God lower the hedge of protection, the defeated one would not hesitate to devour you. Thank God for the hedge! God will protect us at all cost. But we can remove our protection by giving foothold or space to the devil. Remember, any crack or crevice he sees, he'll inch his way in. Jesus wants us focused. He wants us to know who our enemy is. You know how the defeated one gets over on the Body of Christ? Through our ignorance, through a lack of wisdom and understanding.

I've had Christians, Blood washed Christians, to tell me that they did not believe in demons. Now, that's ignorance gone to seed!!! All the evil happenings in this world, and they don't believe in demons or devils? Wow!

Demons are fallen angels who rebelled against God in Heaven. The Word of God declares that one third of the angels were with satan. (Rev. 12:3-4), *"And there appeared another wonder in heaven; and behold a great red dragon, having seven heads and ten horns, and seven crowns upon his heads. And his tail drew the third part of the stars of heaven and did cast them to the earth: and the dragon stood before the woman which was ready to be delivered, for to devour her child as soon as it was born."* These are the angels that left their first estate. Yes, these are the same evil angels (demons/devils), that we will judge. Their job description is to utterly destroy. They will tempt Christians to sin. They have a strong influence especially in this world's system today.

If we give foothold to them, they will depress or oppress us. they are the author of sickness and diseases.

Every tragedy there was and is, was caused by demonic influence and satan was behind it all. But there is a limit on what satan and his demons can do. It's God and God alone that holds the reigns. As I mentioned once before, a Christian can not be possessed by devils. Only where darkness is in that Christian's life, can demons come in (The mind). This is why Jesus is calling us to be focused. We can not be possessed, but remember, we're still in this world's system. Therefore, we can be depressed, oppressed, and harassed by the devil. But, do you know that the greater one lives in us? This means that the devil is subject to us! You've got to know this!!!! God has given us power over every work of the devil. He's given us power over his thoughts, his deeds, and everything else about the defeated one, we have power over.

I don't know about you, but I don't look at things the way I used to anymore. When adversity comes around, I really don't look at the person, I access what's happening and then I can detect what kind of spirit I'm dealing with.

Beloved, this whole warfare business is a Fixed Fight between God and Satan. You see, when you touch a child, you pull at the heart string of that parent. We've got to look at our lives the same way. When the defeated one tugs at us, it's just to slander God. But God will not allow us to be utterly be destroyed! And you can be sure of this: if we prepare for warfare, just prepare, it's not our fight, but just prepare! God will come through because it's His fight!!! and God's going to win every fight! He's going to win simply because He's the Greater One!! Whenever you feel backed in a corner, just stop and settle down and remember; you have power over the enemy because the greater one lives inside of you.(I John 4:4), " *Ye are of God little children, and have overcome them: because greater is He that is in you, than he that is in the world."* The defeated one is only a distractor really. But stay focused and don't take him for granted, for he is a formidable foe. he'll stop at nothing to destroy you, if you let your guard down.

Remember when God told Joshua to go and take Jericho, even the king of Jericho got nervous. You see, when God is moving in your life, your enemy sees it and it makes him nervous.

Because, he knows that whatever God says or does, has already been ordained before the foundation of the world was laid. Now, this may not make sense to you, but nevertheless, here it is: the devil knows he'll never win when it comes to God, but he just doesn't believe it. he figures he can get into the un-regenerated mind of man and slander God before this world, but this is why we're to stay focused!

But getting back to Joshua, God told him to take Jericho. First of all, in chapter one of Joshua, God let Joshua know quite clearly that the battle was not his. No matter what Joshua put his hands to do, God promised to be with him. (Josh. 1:5-7), " *There shall not any man be able to stand before thee all the days of thy life: as I was with Moses, so I will be with thee: I will not fail thee, nor forsake thee. Be strong and of a good courage: for unto this people shalt thou divide for an inher-*

itance the land, which I sware unto their fathers to give them. Only be thou strong and very courageous, that thou to do according to all the law, which Moses my servant commanded thee: Turn not from it to the right hand or to the left, that thou mayest prosper whithersoever thou goest." God let Joshua know that He is the same God that was with Moses. God fought every battle for Moses and Joshua was the General for Moses' armies. He knew what God could do. But he was overcome with grief from Moses' death. He had to be reminded that grieving days are over. It was time to get up and TAKE DOMINION!!!

God told Joshua in 1:6, *Be strong and of a good courage*, then in 1:7, He says again, *be strong and very courageous*, then in 1:9, He says, "Have not I commanded thee? *Be not afraid, neither be thou dismayed; for the Lord thy God is with thee whithersoever thou goest.* We have to be reminded from time to time that we're not fighting our battle. The battle is the Lord's.

It's God's battle and He will go before you and fight and win! But you must prepare. It's something psychological in being prepared. (Focused). God has to have something in the earth to work with.

One of the sons of the prophets died and left a widow and two sons. The woman went before the man of God (Elisha) and told him her husband died and she still owed her creditors. The creditors wanted to take her sons and use them as bondsmen (slaves) to work off the debt. It was bad enough the woman lost her husband in death, but now the creditors were coming to take away her only financial support. The prophet asked her a simple question: What do you have in your house? I want you to see something in this: there will always be something we've got to do or something we need to start with. To bring further clarity to what I'm saying, Adam sinned and gave authority to satan, making it illegal for God to come in the earth even though it was God's creation. (Gen. 1:28), " *And God blessed them and God said unto them, be fruitful and multiply, and replenish the earth, and subdue it: and have dominion over the fish of the sea; and over the fowl of the air, and over every living thing that moveth upon the earth.*

Dominion: a governed territory, rule or power to rule.
Subdue: to conquer; to control

God gave authority to man. Authority over the works of His hands on the earth. Man committed high treason in Eden and sold out to satan. Therefore satan now have dominion. It's illegal for God to come in the earth unless He's called upon in prayer. (II Chron. 7:14) *If my people that are called by my name would humble themselves and pray and seek my face and turn from their wicked ways, then will I hear from heaven, I will forgive their sins and heal their land.*" Look at what happened during the Inter-Testament period (the 400 plus silent years), no one heard from God, because no one called upon Him. When we call on Him, He'll answer. But during this period, everybody was doing their own thing. evil was running rampant in the land. To make a long story short, it's God's battle but what do you have in the house?

Can't nobody take your stuff from the enemy but you

Yes, that's right. Nobody can take your stuff back but you. Often times, if you really check into it, you will find that it was you that gave your stuff away in the first place. Sometimes the devil don't take from us, we give it to him.

We give him opportunity to take our health due to a lack of discipline in our eating habits. Also, we give him our health due to a lack of exercise and taking vitamins like we should. In fact, that's what happened with Adam and Eve. "A lack of discipline in their eating habits." God told Adam to not

touch the Tree of the Knowledge of Good and Evil, because if they did, they would surely die. They ate and We died. All because of a lack of discipline and disobedience.

(Gen. 2:15-17), *" And the Lord God took the man, and put him into the garden of Eden to dress it and to keep it.. And the Lord God commanded the man saying, of every tree of the garden thou mayest freely eat: But of the tree of the knowledge of good and evil, thou shalt not eat of it: for in the day that thou eatest thereof, thou shalt surely die."*

So you see what I mean when I say, we sometimes give our stuff away. Adam gave away his eternal life in the garden. And he gave away ours too, unless we repent of our sins. Thank God for the second Adam!! The first Adam sold us out, but the second Adam bought us back into fellowship with God, Hallelujah!!!

Release the old to walk in the new
Remember Abraham?

Before Abraham could get the stuff God had for him, he had to first release the old. God told him to leave his father, his kindred, leave all that was familiar to him. He had to leave all that he knew in order to get his stuff. Some of yall want your stuff, but you're still holding on to some stuff that mean you no good. Some of yall are sitting in churches that God has told you to leave, yet you're holding on Sunday after Sunday, Wednesday after Wednesday, Friday after Friday, knowing that there is not an ounce of Anointing in the building. But no, you're still sitting up in that TOMB! God been left!!! But you're still there!!! Just because your mama or daddy bought a pew, does not mean you have to be there until the church burn down. Maybe He will allow the church to burn down, then maybe you'll get up out of there! Just get up, LEAVE! The choir is dead, the pastor ain't preaching nothing!...don't study!..no input!, no output!, nothing in!, nothing out!

You see, God moves people or things out of the way in order to get our attention, or He'll tell us to move. When He tell you to leave, don't make up excuses as to why you'll be staying for one more month. It's easy to fall into that, but your Destiny, your Purpose depends on your obedience to God. (Gen. 12:1), " *Now, the Lord said unto Abram, Get thee out of thy country, and from thy kindred, and from thy father's house, unto a land that I will show thee: And I will make thee a great nation, and make thy name great; and thou shalt be a blessing. And I will bless them that bless thee, and curse him that curse thee: and in thee shall all families of the earth be blessed."*

Abram obeyed God immediately, because that fourth verse says, " So Abram departed as the Lord had spoken unto him." But there was a problem right from the beginning: God told him to get away from his kinfolks and he did that except he took Lot (his nephew) with him. And you know the deal about Lot.

When God sends us forth, we can't take everybody with us. If you don't walk alone, you will find yourself in a bind with the kinfolks. Have you noticed that it's the kinfolks that give you the most problems when God is calling you higher? Sometime you have to disconnect yourself from them altogether! I know what I am talking about. Do what you have to do in order to Walk in your Purpose! Get kinfolk out of your business!!!

Remember what Jesus said? A man's foes are of his own household. Tell them all goodbye and walk in your destiny. You will not recover "All" until you do this. Forget about carrying mother, father, sister, brother, and friends with you, because folks carry demonic spirits with them and they will use anybody to stop you! Abram got a glimsp of this, so he left daddy Terah and everybody else, home. Terah was already into baal worship. Joshua refers to Terah's religious practice in (*Joshua 24:2*), " *And Joshua said unto all the people, thus saith the Lord God of Israel, your fathers dwelt on the other side of the flood in old time, even Terah, the father of Abraham, and the father of Nachor, and they served other gods.*

As long as Abram was living around all those different

spirits, there was no way God could call him to be the father of nations. When you're around demonic activity, you don't have clarity of mind. You will find that you just can't be focused. God is about peace, but confusion is of the devil. (I Corin. 14:33), " *For God is not the author of confusion, but of peace, as in all churches of the saints. (James 3:16), " For where envying and strife is, there is confusion and every evil work.*"

That's right, when there are folks around you that's envious of the Anointing that God has placed on your life, separate yourself immediately. Because, it's not going to stop with them just being envious. The Bible says there is also confusion and every evil work. Beloved, even your family will stop at nothing to hinder you from moving higher in God.

I'm prompted by the Holy Spirit to Prophesy to someone in particular: "HEAR THE WORD OF THE LORD: YES, I HAVE CALLED YOU WITH A SPECIAL AND HIGH CALL. AND YOU, LIKE ABRAHAM, MUST GET AWAY FROM CERTAIN FAMILY MEMBERS THAT YOU KNOW ARE HINDRANCES. DON'T FEEL GUILTY, DON'T BE TROUBLED OR DISTURBED ABOUT THIS SEPARATION. FOR THIS IS MY CALL, SAITH THE LORD OF HOSTS. THIS CALL INVOLVES MORE THAN YOU. THE FUTURE OF OTHER SOULS DEPENDS GREATLY ON YOUR MOVE IN THIS CALL. I HAVE CALLED FOUR OTHERS TO FULFILL THIS CALL, BUT THEY WERE MORE CONCERNED ABOUT THEIR FAMILY'S REACTION, THAN MY REACTION. I NOW CALL YOU AS THE FIFTH VESSEL. AND YES, YOU WILL GO AND YOU WILL DO

WHAT I TOLD YOU TO DO, SAITH GOD."

You can not tell everybody your vision. Folks will take your vision and run with it as though God gave it to them, but what they don't understand is that when God called you to do something, He placed and Anointing on you to do that thing. You don't walk in your own power, this is God's call. If He called you, surely He will Anoint you to accomplish the task.

Some of yall need to keep your mouth shut. This reminds me of when I was asked by the editor of a major Christian Magazine to be one of the article writers. I was so excited, I made the mistake and shared this with some folks. Well, need I tell you, I got some looks that sent chills down my spine. I was not boasting, I was just excited about being considered to write for this magazine. I really thought these folks would be excited with me. But no, no, no, immediately I started seeing some stuff. I could write a best seller on that story alone.

So, I decided to keep my mouth shut. When I write articles and when my books and tapes are distributed to the book stores, that's when they'll know about it. Most of these folks are in the Body of Christ and hold the position as "Preacher." You see, I'm just obeying the Holy Spirit. He told me to do my part in getting the Word of God out.

Everybody don't want to see you excel, and they definitely don't want to hear about it. I heard Bishop Noel Jones say: There should be people on your level that you should be able to talk to. These are the people you share little things with. These are the people you confide in.

But, when God start taking you higher in the Anointing and Gifts, these are the people that snare you because they're threatened by your success. So you find yourself alone. So, what you do is, you associate with people that are on a higher level of the Anointing than you are. These are people that are not bothered by your success because they themselves are successful. So, they are not envious of you at all." (I'm talking directly to somebody, I feel you in the Holy Ghost). That's who you start to associate yourself with, people that's not envious of you. It's like crabs in a barrel of boiling water. They can't get out and they will make sure no other crab gets out either!! So learn to keep your mouth shut when God begin to elevate you. If you want to talk to someone, talk to God. Certainly, He's not bothered by your success. In fact, it's God that's causing you to succeed.

When God tell you to leave, don't take Lot with you! Leave him/her at home and move out in God. Yes, walk alone. Tell your husband or wife to keep their mouth shut and you both walk alone. There are times that God need Secret Agents! I hope you're hearing this!!

Don't you know the devil don't want to release your stuff? Don't you know this? This is why when he sees that you are going to move out in God anyway, he'll try to send Lot with you (DISTRACTIONS). So yes, leave Lot home. Don't even share information regarding your call with him/her, because it will be used against you. So what you do is keep your mouth shut.

Remember Isaiah?

Remember what I said earlier, that God will move people out of the way in order to get our attention?

Isaiah didn't even see the Lord until king Uzziah died. Uzziah was in the way of Isaiah walking in his destiny. Isaiah had much to do for the Lord. But he couldn't see the Lord until the Lord moved the king! satan sends so many distractions and king Uzziah was one of them. (Isaiah 6:1), " *In the year that king Uzziah died, I saw also the Lord sitting upon a throne, high and lifted up, and His train (His Glory) filled the temple.*"

When God moved Uzziah, not only did Isaiah see the Lord, but he also saw himself too! He saw the sinner he was. But when you're in the presence of God, you're in the presence of "Absolute Holiness." Therefore, the light of that Holiness will show up the darkness of our sins. (Isaiah 6:5), " *Then said I, woe is me! for I am undone; because I am a man of unclean lips, and I dwell in the midst of a people of unclean lips: for mine eyes have seen the king, the Lord of Hosts.*"

After he saw the Lord in His Glory, he saw himself and all his sins. And, he saw the people that he dwelt with. He saw that they too were in sin and were big liars and back-biters. But, isn't it just like God? He took a liar and made a Prophet out of him! So, this tells me that Isaiah was once a person that you couldn't believe anything he said, but now, you cling to his every word that comes out of his mouth. For you know that he was in the very presence of God, Anointed by God, and sent forth as an awesome Prophet.

After the Seraphims laid the live coal on his mouth,

instead of lying and speaking evil, (let's go there), (Isaiah 6:7-8), " *And he laid it upon my mouth and said, Lo, this hath touched thy lips; and thine iniquity is taken away and thy sin purged (cleansed). Also, I heard the voice of the Lord saying, whom shall I send, and who will go for us? Then said I, here am I; send me."*

Isaiah knew he was ready to stand Holy before the Lord. But, he couldn't stand Holy until Uzziah died. Something old had to be moved before he could even see God. Uzziah (Tradition) was in the way. Tradition is in some of your way too. If you want God's best, you've got to release tradition, if you want your stuff. Remember the Bible said that it was "Tradition" that makes the Word of God of non effect.

Nothing makes me madder or should I say angrier, than when I see a child of God living beneath their privileges. It's common to see this today. Folks go to church, shout, hook-a-messiah, jerk, spit, fall all down on the floor and go home still defeated! They are as broke as ever, and the mind-set is still the same. They name it and claim it, yet nothing changes. Some are still claiming the same stuff they've been claiming for twenty years. Folks just got to wake up and realize God has principles and laws in the earth. And these laws must be obeyed or there will be no harvest. There are also qualifiers in God's Word. (John 15:7), " *If ye abide in me, and my words abide in you, ye shall ask what ye will, and it shall be done unto you."*

You see, the qualifier is: "If my word abide in you (dwells in you), and you abide in my word, then you can ask anything and it shall be done unto you. You know what the most affective prayer is? It's when you learn how to pray the Word of God. Just pray the Word of God. Present God's Word back to Him. That's the Word abiding in you. When you eat and sleep the Word of God, it's abiding in you. When you live the Word of God, it's abiding in you.

You can't Manipulate Him

That's another thing child of God, stop trying to manipulate God. And stop trying to manipulate His People too. Oh, I know I'm talking to somebody now.

There are folks that are walking in the spirit of Jezebel (manipulation and control) while they're in the world, and they come over in the kingdom, saved, but have need of deliverance. Because they bought that same spirit from their old way of living, into their new way of living. And, it wont work. You've got to kill that spirit. God is Sovereign. He knows all things, even our thoughts from afar off. He knows what we're going to think for the rest of our lives and on the day we will think it. Before we form the thoughts in our minds, he already saw it coming in eternity past. He's the Great and Terrible God of the Bible. He's Omni - He's Omnipotent (All Powerful), He's Omniscient (All Knowing), He's Omnipresence (Everywhere at the same time)!!! He's God and there is absolutely nothing impossible to Him. He is Absolute Holiness and Power!

So, you that think you've got it going on with God, and you think He doesn't know you? Think again. He's God.

Don't ever equate Him with man. He is not Synonymous with man. How can He be? He made us! He knows everything there is about us. The body, soul and spirit. Everything man has knowledge of concerning man, God created! And there are yet things about man-kind that we know not of, God created.! He "hears" the lip service we do, but He "listens diligently" to the heart and the motives of the heart. This is why we have to be Holy vessels before the God of Glory. You just can't get over on Him no matter how hard you try. If we want our stuff that the devil is holding hostage, we've got to stand as Holy vessels of Honor before the Lord. You see, Holiness provokes God to move on our behalf, but that spirit of jezebel turns Him off.

THE SPIRIT OF jezebel

When that Jezebel spirit is around, it calls for extreme caution, because this spirit seeks total control. It plays upon and preys upon others with art and skill. It preys upon that are unsuspecting, in order to obtain an advantage over them. Every move this spirit makes is to serve it's own purpose.

When I think about the spirit of Jezebel, I also think about the spirit of humility. You may ask why humility? Well, humility prepares a way of escape from the influence of this spirit. My prayer is that each of us be delivered from the reign of this spirit. This spirit of Jezebel will cause you to dry up spiritually - in God- that is. Those that are walking in this spirit will also cause others to dry up. These people that's under this influence will call on the Anointing of God and the anointing will be gone. God's Anointing is nothing to be played with. God's mercy comes only through the Son. God the Father is not to be played with. Again, His mercy comes only through the Son.

All down through the Old Testament, God had man to present to Him <u>Types</u> of Jesus, so that God the Father would have an avenue to show mercy. The Son of God knows His Father. That's why He's seated on the right hand of the Father making intercession for us. (He*brews 7:25*), " W*herefore He is able also to save them to the uttermost that come unto God by Him, seeing He ever liveth to make intercession for them.*" Jesus is constantly saying, "Father don't consume them for my blood is upon them." And He's going to ever intercede for us "on this side of time." Until the Father says, "Son, go get my children," Jesus will be sitting there pleading our cause.

But we're going to expose this stronghold that's running rampant in the Body of Christ. This spirit is a way of thinking that exists "UNCHECKED" in most churches. We're going to expose some of the hiding places of this devil. (*Rev.* 2:20-21), " *Notwithstanding (nevertheless), I have a few things against thee, because thou sufferest that woman jezebel, which calleth herself a prophetess, to teach and to seduce my servants to commit fornication and to eat things sacrificed unto idols. And I gave her space to repent of her fornication; and she repented not.*

When we speak of Jezebel, we are identifying an "unbridled" witchcraft spirit, a spirit of manipulation, a spirit of control. To understand the spirit of jezebel, we must first go back to the genesis of this spirit. We see jezebel is first mentioned in **I Kgs**. We see this spirit as rebellious and controlling. This spirit operated through queen jezebel which caused more than Ten Million Hebrews, all but seven thousand and one, to bow their knees to baal. This spirit caused most of the Prophets of God to be killed. (I Kgs. 19:14-18), *"And he said, I have been very jealous for the Lord God of Hosts: because the children of Israel have forsaken thy Covenant, thrown down thine altars, and slain thy prophets with the sword; and I, even I only, am left; and they seek my life, to take it away. And the Lord said unto him, Go, return on thy way to the wilderness of Damascus: and when thou comest, anoint Hezael to be king of Syria. And Jehu, the son of Nimshi, shalt thou anoint to be king over Israel, and Elisha, son of Shaphat of Abel-meho-lah, in thy room. And it shall come to pass, that him that escapeth the sword of Hazael, shall Jehu slay: and him that escapeth from the sword of Jehu, shall Elisha slay. Yet, I have left me seven thousand in Israel, all the knees which have not bowed unto baal, and every mouth which hath not kissed him."*

This one spirit was responsible for corrupting and almost destroying an entire nation. That jezebel spirit is ambitious for pre-eminence and control (wanting to be recognized as superior). That name "jezebel" translated, means, "without co-habitation." In other words, this spirit absolutely refuses to live with anyone that it can not control. When this spirit "seems" submissive, it's only to gain a strategic advantage. From the very core of the being of this spirit, it yields to no one.

Keep in mind that the spirit that produced jezebel existed long before the "queen" was ever thought about being born. This spirit came alive in Heaven through lucifer, remember? We refer to jezebel as "she" it's important for you to know and understand that this spirit has " no gender." In other words, there are male jezebels and there are female jezebels.

When this spirit operates through women, it's through women that are bitter towards men. The jezebel spirit is behind the woman that are insecure, jealous, or walking in vanity. They're in bondage and in order to make them feel good about themselves, they will turn around and "bind" you, putting you into bondage. When you see a woman humiliating her husband in public, you're watching the spirit of jezebel at work. With her mouth she controls him through fear of what she might say that will embarrass him. Thus, he goes along with whatever she wants.

This scripture here in Rev. 2:20, the letter John wrote or should I say the letter Jesus wrote to the church of Thyratira: this letter shows this spirit as being immoral, but not only is it immoral, it has a root and reason for operating, and that root and reason is "control," and control is witchcraft. This spirit was sitting in high places and called itself a prophetess. This spirit was strategically set there by the "defeated one" himself. It was set in a high place for the sole purpose of seducing the servants of God. And after seduction, then control. If you have something on somebody and they don't want it exposed, you can twist them around your finger and they will do what you want them to do. Control is what this spirit seeks.

When this spirit operates through men, it's usually that have had problems with their mother. As they were growing up, mom wouldn't let them do this, mom wouldn't let them do that. They found themselves always in the background - no speaking unless spoken to. Mom caused them to operate in fear. These men turn around and marry women just like mom. Thus, pushing themselves further and further in the background of everything and everybody. So, a lot of these men calls themselves prophets or give themselves a high calling (And this calling is not in Christ Jesus either).

By doing this, they feel less intimidated, so they go about intimidating others, manipulating and controlling folks. This spirit was exposed by the

Holy Spirit in the church of Thyratira. It's still walking tall in the Body of Christ today. Don't kid yourself, it's in every church. It's standing tall in your church too, even now. Look around, yes, observe different ones up in your church. You'll spot a lot of them. I've watched it for years in my church. But this spirit must be checked (confronted and stopped).

You see, the defeated one has built a fortress in the spirit realm. Yes, he's built a stronghold at the point it seems natural for some of yall to manipulate and control. I said, it seems natural. But it's not natural, it's a spirit and God Himself will judge it. It's the same spirit in "I Kgs. 21, Naboth had a vineyard close to ahab's palace. And because it was convenient, ahab wanted that piece of land. He wanted to put a garden there. First, he offered Naboth a better vineyard in exchange for his vineyard. Naboth turned him down. The king then offered to buy the land, but Naboth told him, "this is my heritage from my fathers before me. And I have to pass it down to my lineage. "Don't want your money, no matter the price."

The Bible says that ahab was sad and he went into his bedroom and laid down. He couldn't eat or sleep because he wanted that vineyard just that bad. He was so depressed. His wife jezebel came in and saw him in this state of mind, she asked him, "why are you so sad?" He told her the story about Naboth and the vineyard, and the fact that Naboth would not even consider exchanging or selling the land to him. Well, she says, don't you govern all of Israel? Get up! Eat and be merry, I'll give you the vineyard of this Jezereelite, Naboth. I thought, how can you give away something that does not belong to you? This devil wrote letters to the elders and nobles in the city where Naboth lived. She told them to "Set Naboth Up!" She said, "take two of your sons of belial (this name is synonymous with satan, but it also means, no good men or worthless, useless, somebody you can put fear in, somebody that you have something on). Tell them they better say that Naboth blasphemed God and he blasphemed the king too. After you "Trump" these charges, then kill him.

This is an evil spirit and like I said before, when you're in the presence of someone that's walking in this spirit, it calls for extreme caution. This spirit also stirs up strife and has been deposited into the church to shut the mouths of the "True" Prophets and Prophetesses. It's to stop the Word of God that comes out of the mouth of the Anointed of God. But God said, not so. He said, " I have people that are not going to back down from this witchcraft spirit. There are some in the "Body" that may back down, but I've got a few, a few hand-picked servants in my back-pack that will not run like Eligah did.

That war between Eligah and jezebel is still in the church today. But then, the real war is between the demi-gods and the Most High God. And Guess who will "Always Win?" You got it! The Most High God!

Just after Eligah got through call the Fire of God down from Heaven, just because jezebel threatened him, he takes off and run. The message she sent to him was rooted in fear. She sent her messengers to Eligah because he killed her prophets. She said, (paraphrased) " Let the gods do to me, what you did to my prophets, if I don't have your head this time tomorrow. That's what this spirit does, it sprays fear. It has it's roots in fear. And Eligah played right into the hands of this devil. I had a problem with my brother, Eligah. His Destiny, his Purpose was to stop idolatry in Israel. God sent him to cut the head off of this spirit. He started out good. He came "close" to stomping this spirit out. That's what's happening to some of you, you're coming close. But you've got to step into your Purpose, your whole reason for being. Don't allow fear to cripple you. Don't allow control to stop you or even slow you up. Move forward and step into your purpose! Step, Step, Step!!!

When you know who you are, you don't run from fear,

you run towards it, because you Know who's backing you.

Elijah ran all day long into the wilderness. That's a running brother. He ran so, he was exhausted. God, being omniscience, planted a tree in the wilderness because He knew Eligah was coming. Eligah, now exhausted, went to sleep under this tree. The angel in the wilderness, asked him what was he doing under the Sycamore tree. In other words, Eligah, you know

God! You of all people know God has your back. Here you are, running yourself crazy, and now you're asking God to kill you. What's wrong with you? If you'd obeyed God in the beginning and cut the head off of this spirit, you wouldn't be here today asking God to kill you. You "know" the God of Israel, yet you run from jezebel!!!

It took three people to accomplish what God initially asked "one" man to do. Jehu was unstoppable. jezebel was in the palace boasting great things, hollering out the window at Jehu. Jehu went to the palace and said to his servants, "go up and get her and throw her down here." The Bible said she was near death when she hit the ground, but Jehu didn't stop there, he got on his horse and trampled her underfoot, making sure she was dead. Eligah "ran from" jezebel, but Jehu "ran to" her!!! Eligah didn't walk in his purpose. That's why God had to take him out of here before his time!!!

There's something I want you to see in Jehu's spirit that we must possess today in the war against jezebel and ahab: while we must be compassionate towards those that are bound by this spirit, Jehu had no mercy, because there was no hope for reform. He had no sympathy whatsoever towards this demonic spirit. He trampled it underfoot!

Jehu was king, he could have sent his servants to make sure jezebel was killed. But he had a relentless spirit towards the devil. He wanted to make sure the job was done. If you want something done right, do it yourself! He carried out what Eligah was supposed to carry out.

My brother, my sister, "you" fulfill your own Destiny. You make sure that nobody else completes what you are sent to complete. It's "Your" Purpose for being on earth. If you don't fulfill it, then your being born was fruitless. It's never too late to walk in your purpose. It's never too late. So get up and start to walking.

CHAPTER 5

BLESSED BEYOND MEASURE

Webster defines that word "blessed" as follows: Holy, Sacred, Fortunate, Consecrated with Blood, Divine favor, to be endowed with power; marked by God for favor; Positioned to prosper.

When we realize that we are the "blessed" of God, we'll go get our stuff. There is power in that word, "blessed." Once it's spoken, it takes on a personality of it's own. This word "blessed" also has the power of it's own fulfillment. This brings me back to Gen. 25:21. God had already talked to Rebecca (Rebekah), and told her that she was carrying two nations in her womb and that the older would serve the younger. These words were already spoken by God. Words are "alive" and "powerful." When your words are released in the atmosphere, they cause the angels of God to go and bring what was spoken, to pass. If you never "speak" what's yours, you tie the hands of your angels. We've got to keep in mind that God sends angels to minister for us and to minister to us. Angels stand in the presence of God and get what's on the mind of God and ministers to us, what's on His mind.

We have sooo much working on our behalf. We have the Father, Son and the Holy Ghost. We have the angels of God, and we have our "words." God wants us blessed, and not just blessed, He wants us blessed beyond measure. Getting back to Rebekah and her sons, Jacob and Esau: The Bible said that the children struggled within her. And that Jacob came into this world, holding Esau's heel. Too often we find ourselves racing ahead of our time. Not realizing that the blessing has already been ordered and is now "set," and waiting on God's timing. It's fixed! God told Rebekah that the blessing was coming upon the younger. But we see the younger one was trying to be born first. But it was already fixed by God.

Jacob means cunning, slickster. Esau means flaky, and unstable. Esau was a cunning hunter, but that's all he was cunning in. Cunning is defined as skillful and crafty. In order to be cunning, you must be a "thinker," and considering all odds. In other words you've got to be focused and a planner. God wants us thinking. If we're to be blessed beyond measure, we've got to know what to do with our blessing. Believe me, if we're not thinkers, the enemy will come in to play and before you know it your blessing would have dissolved right in your hands. God want us cunning, He wants us focused, and He wants us thinking. If you're thinking clearly, you wouldn't want to be blessed before your time. You would prepare to receive your blessing (faith with works). But, don't force your blessing. Like I said earlier, your blessing has already been fixed by God. Wait on the Lord, and be of good courage. Wait I say, on the Lord. His Word is sound.

It's fundamental to understand Isaiah's emphasis on God's Word. (Isa. 55: 10-11), " *For as the rain cometh down and the snow from heaven and returneth not thither, but watereth the earth, and maketh it bring forth and bud, that it may give seed to the sower, and bread to the eater; So shall my Word be that goeth forth out of my mouth, it shall not return unto me void, but it shall accomplish that which I please, and it shall prosper in the thing that I send it."*

In other words, God's Word has the fulfillment power within itself. So you see, it's a "Done Deal" that you be blessed! God has made many promises throughout Scripture to you. But wait on God.

When Isaac mistakenly blessed Jacob instead of Esau, he could not recall the blessing, for it now existed in "history." His words had acquired an identity all it's own. Blessing and cursing releases a supernatural power which could bring to pass the content of the blessing or the curse.

God gave Moses insight on what He was saying in this benediction. (*Numbers* 6:24-26), " *The Lord Bless thee, and keep thee: The Lord make His face shine upon thee, and be gracious unto thee: The Lord lift up His countenance upon thee and give thee peace."*

In this, God was teaching Moses to teach Aaron how to "Petition and Proclaim" at the same time. He knew the power in that word, "blessed."

Measure is defined as: Dimensions, capacity, a unit; any standard of valuation; a definite quantity measured out; to estimate the extent; a special dimension.

Everything has it's dimensions, and so does everybody. But God says, "I will bless you beyond measure. There are no dimensions in what I will give you and your house. God told Abraham, "I will make of thee a great nation, and I will bless thee and make you a blessing. In other words, I'm going to position you to prosper. And when I position you, you can position someone else. I will bless them that bless you, and I will curse them that curse you. And because of you, shall all the families of the earth be blessed. I'm going to empower you to get wealth. (Gen. 22:17), " *In blessing, I will bless you, and in multiplying, I will multiply your seed as the stars of heaven and as the sand by the sea, so shall your seed be. Your seed shall possess the gates of their enemy. And because you've obeyed my voice, all the nations of the earth shall be blessed because of your seed.*

There was a time when Hagar was expecting Ishmael. Sarai dealth harshly with her and she ran away into the wilderness. The angel of the Lord found her sitting by a fountain in the wilderness. (Guess who put the fountain in the wilderness?) The angel said, "Hagar, where have you come from and where are you going? Hagar answered, I ran from my mistress, Sarai. He said, go back and submit yourself in her hands. Then the angel said to her, I will multiply thy seed exceedingly, at such a multitude, it can't be numbered. You are with child and shalt bear a son and call his name Ishmael, because the Lord hath heard thy afflictions. God even blessed that which was not promised! God went on to say, I will bless Ishmael and make him fruitful and will multiply him exceedingly. Twelve princes shall come from him. But my Covenant, I will establish with Isaac. He is the promised one. Now, God told Abraham, as for Sarai, I want you to call her Sarah, for I have changed her name. Princes shall come from Hagar, but Kings shall come from Sarah. For Isaac is the one that I have chosen for myself. The King of Kings shall come from his loins.

You see, when God speaks, that reality is "right now." It may not look like it, but when the words go forth out of His mouth, they're are then in the birthing process. And the reality of that thing, will be born. God has already promised you as the seed of Abraham, that you are blessed. (Isaiah 55:11), *"So shall my Word be that goeth forth out of my mouth: it shall not return unto me void, but it shall accomplish that which I please, and it shall prosper in the thing whereto I sent it."* God's Word is almighty. His Word is Sovereign. In so many ways, the Eagle reminds me of our God. I did a study some time ago on various birds. I just want to share this with you because I want to see you Soar as an Eagle. You will find that eagles don't move like other birds.

All birds have feathers. And they all have wings. But, they don't all fly. For instance, the Ostrich and Penquin are flightless. Instead of flying, an ostrich walk or run. They use their wings for balance. Penquins swim. They use their wings like flippers. Certain birds serves as symbols. People have long regarded the owl as a symbol of wisdom, and a dove as a symbol of peace. The bald eagle has long represented political and military might. There are about nine thousand seven hundred (9,700) various birds. The smallest is the bee hummingbird which grows only about two inches tall. The largest bird is the ostrich, which grows up to eight feet tall.

Getting back to the eagle: The eagle is a Majestic bird. It has powerful wings and a sharp vision. The eagle is a national emblem and a symbol of the United States. It's an incredible creature in flight. This bird glides effortless through the open skies, commanding the respect of all who looks upon her. What is it that makes this bird so Regal, so Majestic? And why should God compare Himself to the eagle in Scripture? There is obviously something significant about the eagle. We can learn many lessons from this bird. The eagle has been a majestic symbol for centuries. Even during the Roman Empire, the emblem of the eagle was on their shields.

The eagle not only stands for majesty, it's noted for it's strength. The eagle is incredibly strong. For example, an eagle can swoop down from the skies and pick up an animal that weighs more than it does. The eagle is strong. When you do a study on birds, you'll find there to be a multiplicity of birds, but there is "None" like the eagle. I'm sure you've heard the term, "birds of a feather flocks together?" You will never see a flock of eagles.

Eagles, fly alone. They don't share their Majesty! They fly alone. Their strength comes from their wings. The wings of an eagle reaches a wing spread of more than eight feet from tip to tip. No other bird can soar as high as the eagle. No other bird comes close to ascending to great heights like the eagle. They can fly beyond ten thousand (10,000) feet.

You know what? Eagles don't even build their nest like other birds do. An eagle will fly to the highest mountain cliff and build it's nest there. They take extremely large sticks and branches to build their nests. They arrange these branches "IN ORDER" in the cleft of the rock. Then they start to add smaller branches. After this, they line the nest with leaves. And, as a final step, the eagle will take downy feathers that have fallen from their own bodies to cover the inside of the nest. Once the nest is finished, it's very soft inside. Notice where the nest was built: It was built on a rock, a solid foundation. In fact, it is "within" the rock, in the cleft or the crack of the rock.

We're to build our lives on a solid foundation. The foundation is the most important part of any construction, because it's the base. So the foundation "must be" strong.

Notice when Jesus said that a wise man builds his house on a rock, why? Because a rock is one of the strongest foundation anyone can build upon, especially when it's a solid rock. We can take many lessons from the eagle.

The eagle doesn't build an ity bity nest. It builds a nest that is able to withstand the great storms of life. This is a large construction weighing sometimes as much as two tons and well able to weather the elements.

If you know anything about mountains, you know that the strongest gusts of wind usually forms near the peaks of a mountain because of the high altitude. But this nest can withstand the forceful winds because it's built inside of the cleft of the rock. We need to make sure, our foundation is built on the Rock Christ Jesus. You can not build a foundation with knowledge. We've got to get knowledge. Jesus said, "take my yoke upon you and learn of me, learn of me, learn of me. My yoke is easy. My yoke is not like that of the world. My burden is light. Learn, Learn, Learn! (*Hosea 4:6*), "*My people are destroyed for a lack of knowledge. Because you have rejected knowledge, I will reject you, that you shall be no priest to me. Seeing thou hast forgotten the laws of your God, I will also forget your children.* In other words He's saying, you/we embarrass Him, trying to be a priest to Him with no knowledge. God wants us with knowledge so we can soar high like eagles.

IN THE NAME OF JESUS

I'm going to share something else with you. The defeated one does not want you to know of the power that's in the Name of Jesus. Folks go around day after day praying in the name of Jesus. But there is awesome power in that name when you know of the authority you have in that name. We are operating in a spirit world because we are spirit, we live in a body and we have a soul. God is Spirit, and we are created in His likeness. Spirits, angelic and demonic, do not respond to verbiage. They respond to knowledge. Remember the seven sons of Sceva? They wanted to cast out devils, but the devils knew who had power, and they knew that sceva's sons didn't have no power! And they definitely were not qualified to use the name of Jesus! One person may call on the name of Jesus, but with no knowledge of what's in that Name. In this case, little or nothing happens. Another person may call on Him with full knowledge of what's in His Name. In this case, demons trembles and get out of town and satan got to flee too because they're responding now to the knowledge of what's in the Name of Jesus!

When you use His Name with knowledge and understanding of what's in His Name, you can rest assured, something takes place in the heavenlies. We've got to exercise our authority in that Name, Jesus. The early church used the Name "Jesus" like a precisioned tool. (Weapon)

Peter had great revelation of that Name. One thing I've learned about the Hebrew, they attach great significance to their names. They know that you follow the character of your name. Some folks reading this book might need to change their names. (Smile) Look at what God did with Jacob: He changed his name from Jacob, which means "slickster" to Israel, which means "Prince of God." When God changed his name, that's when his character changed. When God confirmed His Covenant with Abram and Sarai, He changed their names. Abram means "Father is exalted," but Abraham means, "Father of a Multitude. Sarai means, "Princess" but Sarah means

"Mother of Kings." When God changed their names, this signified them coming into Covenant with God. They begin to call each other what God called them. So when Sarah called her husband "Abraham" she was saying, "Father of a Multitude." And when Abraham called his wife Sarah, he was saying, Mother of Kings. Yeah, that's how that works, you call it into being. Call that thing that is not, as though it is! They understood the significance behind their names.

Initially, when the Bible was written, there were no such thing as punciation. Punciations were put there by the translators. So when we read (Mark 16:17), *it really should read:* <u>*And these signs shall follow them that believe in my name;*</u> *shall they cast out devils, they shall speak with new tongues; they shall take up serpents; and if they drink any deadly thing, it shall not hurt them; they shall lay hands on the sick, and they shall recover."* The Bible in it's origin did not have punciations. As I said before, the translators put them where they thought they should be.

When you profess Jesus as Savior, you come into Covenant with Him. This gives you authority to use His Name. (After you learn of Him, that is). When we learn what we have in Jesus' Name, the defeated one gets nervous, because he knows then that he has to release your stuff, simply because you know what you're talking about. For he also knows that once your name is written in the Lamb's Book of Life, it's over for him. The Lamb's Book of Life is a record of people that are in Covenant with God. It's like a marriage covenant.

You marry, there is a name change, which means you

are in covenant, and everything that is owned by one, is owned by both. That Name "Jesus" was so necessary in Old Testament times, God provided an avenue by which He could show us Mercy, through that Name Jesus, by providing us with "TYPES AND SHADOWS OF THAT NAME!!!! My God! I hope you see this!!! God has many names throughout Scripture. Most of the names of God are not really names, they are designations, titles. But He has Redemptive Names. They are the names that are revealed by the name "Jehovah." His Redemptive Names reveals the aspect of God's nature and character relative to our deliverance. So throughout the Holy Writ, God begin to reveal Himself through His Names. Let's look at His Redemptive Names:

Jehovah Tsidkenu: The Lord our Righteousness (Jer. 23:6)
Jehovah Mekkadesh: The Lord our Sanctifier (Lev. 20:9)
Jehovah Shalom: The Lord our Peace (Judges 6:24)
Jehovah Shammah: The Lord is There (Eze. 48:35)
Jehovah Rapha: The Lord our Healer (Ex. 15:26)
Jehovah Jireh: The Lord our Provider (Gen. 22:14)
Jehovah Nissi: The Lord our Banner (Ex. 17:15)
Jehovah Rohi: The Lord our Shepherd (Ps. 23:1)

From the Tabernacle of Moses to the Redemptive Names of God, Jesus says, "all of it speaks of me." Through the Law, the Judges, the Prophets, they all prophecy of Jesus. Now it's time for a physical revelation of God. So, the Holy Ghost pulls all this prophecy together in the womb of this little virgin girl, Mary. And this little boy Jesus, grows up, and at the age of thirty years, starts His ministry. Where He sees sickness and diseases, He heals, thus we see Jehovah Rapha. Then He sits with sinners and publicans, we see Him as Jehovah Shammah, the Lord is there. Where He sees the multitude as sheep without a shepherd, He becomes Jehovah Rohi, the Lord our Shepherd. (John 10:11), *I am the good shepherd. The good shepherd give his life for his sheep.* When He sees a storm tossing us to and fro, He becomes Jehovah Shalom, the Lord our Peace (Mark 4:39) Peace be still. Yes, Jesus is all the Redemptive Names of God. God said, "I put my "Word" above my Name. I hope you see this!!!!!!!!!!!!!!! This is awesome. We know that the name Jesus is above every name, but did we know that God put the Name Jesus above "His" Name?????? You've got to see this with everything in you!! So, if you get sick, lay your hands on your own self and say: In the Name of Jesus!! You are then calling on Jehovah Rapha, our Healer. The name of Jesus belong to you. You have a right to that name. That's why Peter and John could tell the lame man that laid daily at the gate called Beautiful, "Silver and Gold have I none, but such as " I have" give I thee, in the name of Jesus Christ of Nazareth, rise up and walk. See, they knew what they had. I love it that they said, "Jesus Christ of Nazareth," because during that time, there were several Jesus', but they made it plain which Jesus they were talking about. They knew the power that is in that name. (Acts 3:1-9; 13-16). All power is in the name of Jesus. And if you don't know that, the devil does. That's why the defeated one tried to stop the disciples from preaching and teaching in the name of Jesus.

The defeated one knew he had to get out of town when that name was used by a person that had full knowledge of the power and authority that is in that name. Look at that the devil did: he used the Sadducees, Scribes, Caiphas, and Alexander - all rulers. They brought Peter and John to court after they'd locked them up for healing the lame man. The rulers asked Peter and John, by what power or what name have you done this? Peter spoke up, of course. He said, "Be it known unto you all, and to all the people of Israel that by the Name of Jesus Christ of Nazareth, whom you crucified, whom God raised from the dead, by him does this man stand before you today. This is the stone that you threw away. He is now the head of the corner.

Neither is there Salvation in any other Name under Heaven given among men, whereby we must be saved. When they saw the boldness of Peter and John, they marveled and realized they had been with Jesus. With the man standing there that had been healed, they couldn't say anything against it. So they told Peter and John to go outside of the court room. And the Bible said the rulers took council (or should I say, the devil took council with his demons). They said among themselves, there is no doubt a notable miracle has taken place by them. And it's manifested for everybody to see. We can not deny it. But we're going to make sure that this go no further than Jerusalem.

We're going to threatened them that they speak no more to nobody in "that Name." So they called Peter and John back into the court room and commanded them not to speak anymore or teach anymore in the Name of Jesus. But Peter answered, "I've got to listen to God and not you! The rulers threatened them again and let them go. Peter and John went to their own and told their people all that the chief priest and elders had said to them. Do you think Peter and them made plans to obey the rulers? I DON'T THINK SO! This only made them even more determined to preach and teach in the Name of Jesus. When they went back to their people, Peter said, "let's pray." This is the prayer he prayed: And now Lord, they've threatened us. Grant unto us, your servants, the boldness to speak and stretch forth your hand to heal, and that signs and wonders may be done by the name of the Holy One, Jesus.

The Bible said that when they prayed, the place where they were, begin to shake. And they were all re-filled again with the Holy Ghost and they spoke the word of God with boldness.

If you don't know already, get to know what's in that Name, Jesus. It's Awesome!!!! Once you "see" this, you can just reach right into the enemy's camp and pull your stuff out. It's as easy as that.

DELIVERED FROM PEOPLE

Before I go any further under this subject, I want you to know I am sharing some of this information with you from Bishop Noel Jones.

That's right!!! You need strength to go into the enemy's camp. People will drain you of every ounce of strength if you let them. This is why it's Prudent to walk alone. I'm going to share this with you: satan has a reprobated mind. he is reprobate!!! he is corrupt in all his ways. he's depraved, he is evil and he knows how to destroy or cripple something Holy and Pure, because he messed himself up! he was once holy and pure. If he defiled himself, who do you think you are that he wont use you?

My sister, my brother, you can be Saved, Sanctified, and filled with the Holy Spirit, but if you are not SOBER, he'll corrupt you and he'll use you to corrupt someone else. he is reprobate! he is without hope of Salvation, and guess what? he doesn't want Salvation, now or ever. But what he wants to do is tear your salvation down. he wants anybody that's holy, pure, and praises God. he hates everyone that truly serves God. he will do all he can to try and destroy your relationship with God. And he has committed himself to the lake of fire to do it. PLEASE HEAR ME: he is like a roaring lion seeking whom he may devour. he comes to church "seeking." he'll go right up on the choir, "seeking." he'll go up in the pulpit, "seeking" whom he may devour. The defeated one has nothing to lose and he is serious about your destruction!

He's not at all concerned that you are in church. he's seeking to destroy you right up in the house of prayer. And he'll send someone up in there to tear you down.

You better hear me child of God!! This is an urgent call for your undivided attention. satan has nothing to lose because he is already defeated.

There are times when God will seclude you from people. Because people, even at their best, don't always bless you. Sometimes, well meaning people can cause you much pain. You could be experiencing an accusation. There could be people around you that know you are right about an issue, they will know you're right, and will not back you up because of the influences of other people. God has to separate us from people. Sometimes, you may find yourself around such negative folks that everything they say will draw from you instead of strengthen you. So instead of having you fed with negative things, God will separate or isolate you from these people. Some of your friendships, the devil didn't break them up, God did it! Some of your family relationships, God put division there, not the devil. God knows "ALL" and He sees the motives of their hearts. So rather than have you hurt or injured, God severs the relationship. Blood ain't got nothing to do with it, it's the motives of their hearts that God is protecting you from.

Yeah, people will know that you're right , they will know the truth and sit there and wont say anything on your behalf.

All they have to do is speak up and the devil will have to flee. But they wont do it because of other influences. People have a tendency to be with you when you're up. But when they feel you're going down, you'll look around and find yourself alone. satan will use people to test you. Folks will cause you to cry alllllllll night long. If you think about it, most of your self-esteem problems, most of the pain you encounter, is either because of a person, or people. Most of your struggles in prayer, most of your fights to live Holy, (to walk with God), are about people. Your greatest fight in this life is because of people. People will test your relationship with God. People will put you in a situation, they will "Set-You-Up, and then they'll walk off and they'll Watch! They will watch. They will watch to see how you will handle the trap that they set up for you.

Preachers, this is for you: Always be conscious of who you serve. Always serve those who need you. And, always forget the opinions of your co- laborers. A preacher must never preach to his/her fellow co-laborers, but preach to the folks out in the audience. You will never be as affective to your co-laborers, as you will be to the people of God in the audience. Why? Because most of your co-laborers have a greater problem with your ministry <u>because</u> he/she is a co-laborer, than the people you minister too. Envy does not begin with the people you serve, rather it begins with the fellow co-laborers who serve with you.

Jesus' greatest problems didn't come from the people He served, His problems came from the people that were serving before He got there. (Pharisees and Sadducees) They had the respect of the people until Jesus came on the scene. They were so awed by the miracles of Jesus and how He blessed the people, yet they wouldn't help Jesus bless the people. So they sought to kill our Lord because they didn't have His notoriety.

Some people get close to you, and it appears it's going to be a great relationship at first. But you find out they're just getting close to you to see what you're about. The more they find out about you, the more they dislike what you're about. People will hate you just for the dream you have for yourself.

They'll hate you for the vision God gave you and they'll hang with you long enough to see if it's really going to manifest. But then they think, maybe your vision is going to make a fool out of you and they'll be there for the laugh. Even though they're smiling in your face. Some folks are hanging with you, hoping you never achieve your dream/vision. And, they'll stay close by you just in case you might achieve. (but, they'll do all they can to make sure you wont).

When God change your direction (and He does change our direction), whenever He change your direction, you're going to "squeeze" somebody. I say this because whenever God moves you, there will be traffic in the way. If God's Hand was on everybody that hang with you, if they give in to the Will of God, when God moves you, they would have moved too! So God's traffic control don't cause congestion. But, because everybody is not being moved by God, when God moves you, it leads to conflict because some folks are being moved in your way by the devil, who has been peeping your direction and he's trying to stop you from getting there. **To do God's Will, you've got to be released and deliv-**

ered from people!!!!!!!

You can not be bound by people and get to where God wants you to go. That's why the woman, after twelve years, had to forget people. She had to press her way through the crowd to get what her faith said belong to her. And if you don't have the nerve to "Press" over people, you'll never get your stuff back from the defeated one. You've got to learn how to praise God in spite of people. You've got to learn how to lift Him up, in spite of people. You've got to learn how to walk with Him, in spite of people. You've got to learn how to hold on to Him, in spite of people. The devil don't want you to have anything, and he got some folks out here that don't want you to have anything!!!

Often times, people are with you and around you, and they don't <u>show their hand.</u> They don't show their hand because they're not sure whether or not it's the right time to expose their hand. You can be around folks that you **never thought** that it was **that muchVenom in them against you,** until somebody else tried to take you out and they thought you were through and they showed their hand.

People don't show their hand when you're up. They show their hand when you're in the middle and it looks like you're going down. They figure you're dead now, but then, instead of going all the way down, God catches you before you hit bottom and turns you back upward. Now, those folks don't know what to do! God will put them in a position where they don't know what to do! They don't know whether they should call you, or leave you alone. They don't know whether they should ask you to forgive them, or just go on about their business and just don't show up no more. They don't know what to do! If that doesn't prove that God is with you, I don't know what does.

If God saves you from anything in life, He's going to have to save you from people. One of the ways God delivers you from people is to fix it so you wont need anything they've got. People can really be trying sometimes.

People will hang with you, but you soon find out that they're hanging with you is not about you, it's about them. They'll suck you until you're dry. And when you're left with nothing, they're satisfied.

You'll get in more trouble with people over what you believe God for, more than He has already done. I say this because one Sunday morning I was in a vision. And I heard the Holy Ghost say, "after you retire, you're going to need a jet because I'm going to open **that** many doors for you to minister. Well, I made the mistake and shared that with someone I thought was close to me (a preacher too). The response was: What is your problem? Who do you think you are? Wow! I didn't take it any further because I could see where that was going. I didn't even respond. Folks will **"Lose it"** on what you believe God for or what God told you He was going to do. That's why a lot of us have not been able to speak what we believe God will do, because folks begin to judge us on what has not even happened yet. This is why God shuts us off from people.

Sometimes you can't understand why some relationships just "crash." You can't understand why the person you looked up to the most "Crushed" you so hard. Some of you are wounded by people you trusted your everything to. And you believed if anybody was for you, they would be. And they systematically crushed all your expectations and hopes. God taught you right then and there that the only person that mean you complete and total blessing is God. That's right. Put your trust totally in God. Never in man because man will fail you every time. As a matter of fact, you will fail yourself. So put your trust only in God for He is the only one that cares for you unconditionally.

CHAPTER 6

THE PRESENCE AT WORK (ON YOUR BEHALF)

He is forever at work on your behalf, to direct you, to prompt you to go into the enemy's camp and take all that the devil stole from you. He's so Awesome, I just want to talk about Him a little bit, do you mind? I didn't think you'd mind.

Of course the Presence is the Holy Spirit. He has not come to talk about or demonstrate who He is, in fact "Holy Spirit" is not a name, it is a title, it is a designation. This let me know that He withheld His name in order that the name of Jesus be Glorified. That's right, whenever we glorify Jesus, we can be sure the Holy Spirit is on the scene. Oh yes, whenever Jesus is exalted, you can be sure the Holy Spirit is in the building. We don't have to pump Him up, because He is the Power of God.

We don't have to shout Him up, because He is the Power of God. We have sooo much to learn about Him. The Body of Christ is living far beneath it's privileges.

All we have to do is walk Holy and Exalt Jesus, Glorify Him! And how do we glorify Jesus? (John 15:8), " *Herein is my Father glorified, that ye bear much fruit; so shall ye be my disciples.*

In the second chapter of Acts, shortly after Pentecost, the men were accused of being intoxicated. There were seventeen nations represented at Pentecost in Jerusalem. And, they each heard their language coming from the men and women of God. The Bible said they mocked God's people and accused them of being drunk. But, Peter stood up and lifted up his voice and begin to set the matter straight. (Acts 2:14), " *But Peter standing up with the eleven, lifted up his voice, and said unto them, ye men of Judea, and all ye that dwell at Jerusalem, be it known unto you, and hearken to my words: but these are not drunken as ye suppose, seeing it is but the third hour of the day. But this is that which was spoken by Joel the Prophet....*" The point is, Peter stood up and he lifted up his voice.

When he did this, he became a witness on earth to what was happening in Heaven. We've got to do this too in order to be a witness. We've got to first stand up, then we can lift up Jesus.

The Holy Spirit has sooo many names, but one of my favorites is, "The Presence." He is a mystery to so many Christians. He is the unseen member of the Trinity. Very few believes understand who He is, or the vital role He plays in helping us. Yes, He is the Paraclete, the one who comes along side us to help us. He is ever present in the world today. This is not a complete study on Him, but I'm just sharing basic knowledge of Him, His ministry and His purpose. As you get to know Him, you'll have a new appreciation for Him. He is ever present, (Omnipresent), every where at the same time. (Ps. 139:7-10), *"Whither shall I go from thy presence? If I ascent up into Heaven, thou art there: If I make my bed in hell, behold, thou art there. If I take the wings of the morning, and dwell in the uttermost parts of the sea, even there shall thy hand lead me, and thy right hand shall hold me.*

Some of you may ask, "Just who is this Holy Spirit anyway?" He is the third Person of the Godhead. He is the Arm of God. He is the Hand of God. He is God's Presence. When God speaks, He is the one that goes and bring it to pass. In the book of Beginnings, whenever you see, "And God said let there be," He is the one that brought everything into manifestation. After God finish saying, "Let there be," His next step was to start "creating." Yes, the Holy Spirit was always there (Jehovah Shammah - The Lord is there). He was there in the Beginning. In fact, before the beginning began, He was there. He is God. He is Eternal, He has no beginning and He has no ending. God is just "IS!" Let's give Him Praise and Glory for who He is!!! He is the "I AM." When Moses was on Mt Horeb, and saw the bush burn but not consumed, God called him out of the bush. Well, during their conversation about Moses going back to Egypt to get the Hebrews from Pharaoh, Moses knew that the Hebrews had acclimated to their surroundings in Egypt.

He knew that they were serving the gods of the Egyptians. They had thousands

of gods. They had a god for everything. A god for sleeping, a god for being awake, a god for walking, a god for talking, etc.

All of these gods got their power from their main god (the sun god) that goes by the name of "rah." Moses knew that they would ask the name of this God. God told Moses to tell them that "I AM" has sent you. And I Am "that" I Am. He's saying I Am all you need me to be.

It was the Presence of God (The Holy Spirit) that set the rainbow in the sky as a token of a covenant between God and Noah (the earth), that there will never again be a flood that would destroy the whole earth, that there would never again be a flood that would destroy all flesh. It was the Holy Spirit that ministered to Noah in how to build the Ark. It's amazing that He had Noah to put a window in the "ceiling of the ark." And He told Noah, "You don't even have to lock the door. I am going to lock the door from the out-side. This let me know that the Holy Spirit knew that Noah would look out of the window and see the faces of folks he knew and loved, and be tempted to open the door and let them in. Now, Noah couldn't see out of the window, and he couldn't open the door.

It was the Holy Spirit that caused Sarah's reproductive organs to quiver with life, after she was of old age. To gather some understanding of the Holy Spirit, you would have to abandon your faculty of reasoning, for He is Supernatural. Yes, there has to be a death to your reasoning in order to see Him. Most of the time when He was ministering in the Old Testament times, you would see the Power side of Him. But, He is also very Vocal. He speaks to our spirit. Spirit to spirit! Deep calleth unto deep!

Each member of the Godhead have their own separate character. Once, I asked the Holy Spirit, " Holy Spirit, what's the difference in the character of the Father, the Son, and You?" He answered, "Well, the Father will not tolerate sin. He love the world (man) through the Son. But, He is the epitamy of Holiness, and can not tolerate the least of sin. Jesus, the Son, hates sin too. That's why He came and died. He's Merciful. The Father shows His mercy through the Son. That's why He had to have "Types and Shadows" of Jesus in the earth before Jesus came in the flesh. This provided an avenue for God's mercy on earth or in the earth (man) until Jesus came bodily. As for Me, He says, I can not tolerate sin either.

Where sin is, I am hindered from fulfilling my ministry in a person's life. Through the mercy of the Father, I will remain through the Son, but if the person continues in sin, the Father releases me to leave. Awesome! Awesome! Awesome! I marvel at some of the differences in their characters, Three, but yet One.

Everything regarding the Holy Spirit in the New Testament is already found in the Old Testament, with one exception, the word, "Baptize." You'll notice in the Old Testament times, no one was ever baptized in the Holy Spirit. That was because He had not yet come in the Fullness. So, in the Old Testament, He would "Rest upon" the Kings, Prophets, Priests, Judges, directing them in the ways of the Lord. But when Jesus came and ascended and sent Him back in the fullness (or rather a measure of the fullness as Jesus is the only one that has the fullness of Him), then man could be baptized in Him.

As Jesus told the Samaritan woman at the well about the Water that shall be in her. (John 4:13-14), *"Jesus answered and said unto her, whosoever drinketh of this water shall thirst again, but whosoever drinketh of the water that I shall give him, shall never thirst; but the water that I shall give him, shall be in him a well of water springing up in everlasting life."* Jesus also mentioned in (John 7:37-39), *"In the last days, that great day of the feast, Jesus stood up and cried saying, If any man thirst, let him come unto me and drink. He that believeth on Me as the Scripture hath said, out of his belly (his innermost being) shall flow rivers of Living Water. But this spake He of the Spirit, which they that believe on Him should receive: For the Holy Ghost was not yet given; because Jesus was not yet glorified."* Yes, when Jesus was Glorified, He sent the Holy Spirit back to help us. He is a keeper, in fact, He is "The" keeper.

When Jesus was risen from the dead, He came to where the disciples were hiding for fear of the Jews. Jesus came in the midst of them. (John 20:21-22), *"Then said Jesus to them again, Peace be unto you. As my Father hath sent me, even so, send I you.*

And when He had said this, He breathe on them and saith unto them, Receive ye the Holy Ghost." You will note that this was not the initial in filling. Keep in mind, they were fearful and hiding. Jesus knew they needed power to be kept until the day of Pentecost was "fully come." So He breathe on them that they receive a "measure" of the Holy Spirit. This measure was to strengthen them, to keep them, and give them His Peace. Please recall in John 20: Jesus said, "Peace be unto you three times." The Breath of God is life to us. "Breath" is another symbol of the Holy Spirit. He's Awesome! (Isaiah 40:13), *"Who hath directed the Spirit of the Lord or being His counselor hath taught Him?"*

In Old Testament times, He's considered more of the "Power" rather than the Person of God, because He works as the Divine Agent rather than a distinct Personality. Can you imagine this kind of power on your side? Well He is!!!

The somewhat mysterious Third Person of the Godhead through whom God "Acts" reveals God's Will, empowers individuals and discloses His Personal Presence in Old Testament and New Testament.

OLD TESTAMENT

The name "Holy Spirit" is found only in *Psalms 51:11 and Isaiah 63:10-11,* but reference to the Spirit of God however, is abundant. One of His attributes is "Wind." God uses this Agent in two ways: As an Awesome destructive force that divides the red sea, and as a force to dry up the bottom of the sea so Israel could walk through on dry ground. Of the "Eighty-seven" times that the Holy Spirit is described as "Wind," Thirty-seven describes the Wind as the agent of God, ever strong and intense. This agent of

God clearly reflects the power of God.

Another quality of the Holy Spirit is His mysteriousness (Ps. 104:3). This demonstrates that the Holy Spirit operating as "Wind" is able to transport God on His wings to the outer limits of the earth. No one can tell where the Wind has been, and no can tell where He's going. He is God!

In the Old Testament, there are numerous examples where in the Prophets were inspired by the Holy Spirit. The "Judges" are accredited with being inspired by the Holy Spirit as in Othneil, (Judges 3:10). Sometimes, the Holy Spirit would rest mightily upon certain individuals to the point of altering their normal behavior. (I Sam. 10:16;19:23-24).

NEW TESTAMENT

The Spirit inspired Prophet's voice returned after four-hundred plus years of silence. When John the Baptist came on the scene the coming kingdom of God, Zechariah and Elizabeth were informed that John would be filled with the Holy Ghost even from Elizabeth's womb. (Luke 1:15). The Angel Gabriel, visited Mary with the news that the Holy Ghost shall come upon her and overshadow her, and that the Holy thing which shall be born of thee, will be called the Son of God. (Luke 1:35).

Jesus was anointed by the Holy Spirit. He was led into the wilderness by the Holy Spirit to be tempted of the defeated one (Luke 4:1-13). Luke has more reference to the Holy Spirit than any of the Synoptic Gospels. Look at this too: All of the Apostolic writers witnessed the

Holy Spirit in the Church. But, it was the Apostle Paul that offered the most theological reflection on the subject. (*Rom.* 8; *Icor.*2:12-14; II *Cor.* 3; *and Gal.* 5).

His Personality

He's a person, therefore, He has a personality. To believe in His personality is a pre-requisite to belief in the Trinity. His characteristics alone entitles Him to be considered personal. A real person is not physical body (what you can see and touch), but the spirit and soul within the body. He is often described in an impersonal way as the "Unction, the Fire, the Water. These are mere descriptions of what He does. The basic office of the Holy Spirit is that of Comforter. Jesus mentions this in (John 14:16). He's the Author, (II *Tim* 3:16), "*All Scripture is given by inspiration of God...* He is Teacher and Guide, (John 14:26), " He shall teach you all things...He's a witness to Christ. (John 15:26) *He shall testify of me.* He is Creator, (Ps. 104:30) *Thou sendest forth thy Spirit, they are created.*

His chief office is Comforter. And when you're comforted, you're comforted by a person. When Jesus said that the Holy Spirit was going to replace Him on earth, a Personal Spirit had to fulfill that job. He is referred to in the male gender. Jesus said, *He shall glorify me; for He shall receive of mine and show it unto you.* (John 16:14). In this sixteenth chapter of John, the masculine pronoun is used "Twelve times" when referring to Him. John records our Lord's words on other occasions: (John 14:17), "*But you know Him: for He dwelleth with you and shall be in you.*"

Common characteristics of a person is intellect, emotion, and will. And the Holy Spirit has each of these attributes. His intellect (I Cor. 2:10), *For the Spirit searcheth all things, yea, the deep things of God." (Rom. 8:27) "And He that searcheth the heart, knoweth what is the mind of the Spirit, because He maketh intercession for the saints."* He's concerned about our language. He's very concerned about "how" we speak. (Acts 2:4), *"They began to speak with other tongues, as the Spirit gave them utterance."* He exercises His will. (I Cor. 12:11), *"But all these worketh that one and the self same Spirit, dividing to every man severally as He will."* He Wills! He has desires and preferences. (Rom. 8:27), *" And God who searches our innermost being, knows what is preferred by the Spirit...* He chooses according to His will.

Even though He exercises His will, it is "Always" in cooperation and harmony with the Father and the Son. (I John 5:7) *There are three that bare record in Heaven, the Father, the Word, and the Spirit, and these three are one."* They have separate and distinct personalities, but they are yet "One."

Most folks find int difficult to comprehend the personality of the Holy Ghost. We know that He will not be identified with theophanies (physical appearance or personal manifestation), but we do know when He's in the house!!! He's present in this world today in an Awesome way. He comes with so much to offer the Body of Christ. My brother, my sister, I introduce you to God's Presence.

The Presence in Salvation

He's present in Salvation to convince you that you are saved, that you are born again, that you are brand new. He's here to let you know that your blood line has changed. In other words, He's here to tell you, that you have a new daddy. Yes indeed, your DNA has changed! And no earthly research can determine your destiny in Him, only Heaven can!!!! Yes, He's present in salvation, but there's much more to Him than that. Remember, we're talking about the very presence of God Himself. You experience Him in salvation, but there's another experience following salvation, and that is called being Filled with the Holy Spirit, which leads to the Baptism in Him. (Acts 8:14), *"Now when the Apostles which were at Jerusalem heard that Samaria had received the Word of God...* Now, these people had just received the Word of God, (already saved), and the Apostles knew that they were saved. This is why they sent for Peter and John to come to Samaria and pray that the new convert be filled with the Holy Ghost. And when Peter and John laid hands on them, they received the Holy Ghost. Why did Peter and John come? Why didn't Phillip lay hands on them? He was the Evangelist of the hour? Well, child of God, we don't all walk in the same level of Anointings.

You may ask the question, Well, how did folks know that Samaria received the Holy Ghost? The answer is: The "evidence" was there. They spoke in tongues as the Spirit of God gave them utterance.

Not only that, the other people of Samaria saw and heard them speak. That's one of the reasons judas' father, simon the sorcerer wanted the Holy Ghost. he saw and heard something that made him desire the Holy Ghost. (Acts 8:9).

At first he wanted to buy the this power. (Acts 8:18-19), *" And when simon saw that through laying on of the Apostles' hands the Holy Ghost was given, he offered money, Saying, give me also this power, that on whomsoever I lay hands, he may receive the Holy Ghost."* Remember, he at one time was a sorcerer. Even the devil has to recognize when God comes on the scene. Oh yes! The Presence of God sometimes flaunts Himself. I love it! Some folks in the church have yet to catch hold and hook up to Him. What they call the Anointing, is really emotion. He's at work in the earth for us, and some of us are missing Him! He has much to offer! Without Him helping us, we would never get our stuff back from the defeated one. He is the Revealer. He will show you what's happening that's keeping you from getting your stuff back.

Simon the sorcerer, was not the only one that heard and saw the Power of God move. If you go over to the tenth chapter of Acts to Cornelius's house, his entire family received the Holy Ghost. (He was a gentile, but he gave often for the work of the ministry). This is why God remembered him and his house. (Acts 10:44-46), *" While Peter yet spake these words, the Holy Ghost fell on them which heard the words. And they of the circumcision which believed, were astonished, as many as came with Peter, because that on the gentiles also, was poured out the gift of the Holy Ghost. For they heard them speak with tongues and magnify God."* So you see, when He comes on the scene everyone will know beyond a shadow of a doubt that He's in the house!

When the "Presence" made His entrance in the earth, "In the Fullness," He came bearing fruit and gifts. No, He didn't come empty-handed. He brought

Fruit and Gifts to and for us. Well, He only mimicked the Father and the Son. Our Father gave us gifts in the Old Testament times. He gave the Kings, Prophets, Priests, Judges and Pastors. The Son gave gifts to the church too. (Eph. 4:11), *"And He gave some, Apostles; and some, Prophets; and some, Evangelist; and some, Pastors and Teachers, for the perfecting of the saints, for the work of the ministry, for the edifying of the body of Christ; till we all come in the unity of the faith and of the knowledge of the Son of God, unto a perfect man, unto the measure of the stature of the fulness of Christ."*

When the Holy Spirit came, He brought with Him Fruit and Gifts. (The Fruit of the Spirit). The Fruit mentioned here denotes the very Character of Jesus. We are to model the Fruit that the Holy Spirit brought to the Church. In doing this, we become more and more like Jesus. And, I believe that is God's ultimate goal for the church on earth.

For if we love the brethren, we will have the Joy and Peace of the Lord. We must be Longsuffering and be gentle with one another. We are to walk in faith, wavering nothing. We are to be meek with the Sword of the Spirit in our hands, (Word of God). Yet, we are to still walk in temperance, (self control). Jesus was all this as He stood before Pilate. He being God, knew that the Father had His back in every decision He made. And, He'd made up His mind in Gethsemane, that He was going to "Finish" the work He'd started.

We were on His mind. He knew we couldn't come to the Father, if He didn't go to Calvary. Remember, He told Peter in Gethsemane, when Peter drew his sword, "Peter, if I call on my Father right now, He'll send me twelve legions (72,000) of Angels to take me out of here., but for this cause I came into this world. We are to walk as Jesus walked. We are to talk as Jesus talked. I stand in Awe every time I think of Jesus standing in the judgement hall of Pilate, alone, but yet, not alone, for the Father was with Him to a point. To the point where He became "sin," then the Father had to turn His back. But, guess who was there all the time? You guessed it. The "Presence," the Holy Ghost of God never left Him. That's who was keeping Him. They beat Him, they spit on Him, slapped Him and plucked out His beard, yet He just stood there, not saying anything on His behalf. Now, that's temperance.

The Flow Of The Presence

He is the Executive Power of God. Our Father completed His job in planning Salvation. The Son came down and completed His Redemptive work. He is now sitting on the right hand of the Father in the throne of God, making intercession for us. The hour in which we now live is the age of the Holy Spirit. We're living in the hour that God, through the mouth of Joel spoke of. (Joel 2:28-29), " *And it shall come to pass afterwards, that I will pour out my Spirit upon all flesh; your sons and your daughters shall prophesy, your old men shall dream dreams, your young men shall see visions: And also, upon the servants and upon the handmaidens in those days will I pour out of my Spirit.* Peter quoted Joel in Acts 2:14-18).

Yes, the Spirit of God was poured out and He begin to flow among the brethren and the sisteren too! The Word of God declared that there were women and the mother of Jesus "already praying" in the upper room when the men came in. The same thing is happening today. We, the women of God is already in prayer, in fact, our praying is what caused the men to come in. Thank God for the praying men!

Now, back to His flow: (Eze. 47:1-5, 8-8) Ezekiel saw the throne of God in God's great house. Out from the throne of God flowed a river of life. Ezekiel said, " Afterwards, He brought me again unto the door of the house eastward: for the forefront of the house stood towards the east, and the waters came down from under the right side of the house, the south side of the altar. Then He brought me out of the way of the gate northward, and led me about the way without who the utter gate by the way that looketh eastward; and behold there ran out rivers on the right side. And when the man that had a line in his hand, went forth eastward, he measured a thousand cubits, and he brought me through the waters; the waters were to the ankles.

Again, he measured a thousand, and brought me through the waters, the waters was to the knees. Again, he measured a thousand and brought me through: And the waters were to the loins.

Afterwards, he measured a thousand; and it was a

river that I could not pass over: for the waters were risen, waters to swim in. A river that could not be passed over. Then said he unto me, these waters issued out towards the east country and go down into the desert and go down into the sea: which being brought forth into the sea, the waters shall be healed. And it shall come to pass that everything that liveth which moveth whithersoever the rivers shall come, shall live. And there shall be a great multitude of fish, because these waters shall come thither: for they shall be healed. And everything shall live whither the river cometh. These are the rivers of God flowing. This is the Holy Spirit. (John 7:38-39), " *He that believeth on me, as the scripture hath said, out of his belly shall flow rivers of living waters. (But this spake he of the Spirit, which they that believed on Him should receive: for the Holy Ghost was not yet given; because that Jesus was not yet glorified."*

Jesus told the disciples that they would know when He reached Heaven, because when He got back there, He was going to send back the Holy Spirit. (John 16:7).

Remember, the atmospheric heaven is where demonic powers abode or lives. Jesus made an open show of them when He ascended, by going right through their home town. "Smile" Not only did He go through their home, but He led captivity captive, (all those that died in the Lord), He led them through too, smile. Before He left, He made a promise to the disciples that He was not going to leave them comfortless. He promised to send back the Holy Spirit, the Presence of God.

I'm sure lying devils whispered to the disciples, "He's not going to make it back, He lied to you. He ain't sending nobody back here for you. He came and taught you and left you alone. But Jesus had already showed them that He is not a liar. He'd already demonstrated to them His power. Somebody remembered what Jesus said in (Luke 24:49), " And behold, I send the promise of my Father upon you: but tarry (wait) here in the city of Jerusalem until ye be endued with power from on high." (Acts 1:4-B), " ...but wait for the promise of the Father which saith He, ye have heard of Me. For John truly baptized with water; but ye shall be baptized with the Holy Ghost not many days hence (from now). But ye shall receive power after that the Holy Ghost is come upon you: and ye shall be witnesses unto me both in Jerusalem, and in all Judea, and in Samaria, and into the uttermost part of the earth." (Acts 2:1-4), " And they were all filled with the Holy Ghost and begin to speak in other tongues as the Spirit of God gave them utterances." (Act 2:3), " And there appeared unto them cloven tongues (split tongues) like as of fire, and it set upon each of them."

These Scriptures let us know, or should I say they confirm that Jesus made it back to the Father.

The day of Pentecost was the beginning of that river flowing (the river that Ezekiel spoke about). It was a river of tongues with power from on high. To my beautiful catholic brothers and sisters: the Blessed Mother was among the men and women at Pentecost. And she "spoke" and "prayed" in tongues too. It's in the Word of God. Tongues are the languages of the Holy Ghost. He knows how to teach us how to flow in Him.

After the disciples were endued with the power of the Holy Ghost, they went about healing the sick, speaking words of deliverance and wholeness to the world. They could do this because they flowed in the Holy Spirit. The rivers of healing power flowed through them to touch this dark evil world. This river of God, is some what like the Great Mississippi river. The Mississippi river was damned up. And when it broke free and flooded many towns and cities, it was just reclaiming it's territory. It was where it was supposed to be. It had been damned up by man, but now the great Mississippi river said, " I'm Back! The Holy Ghost is saying to the church world, "you tried to shut my mouth when you allowed satan to enter your minds and start denominations. You tried to shut my mouth when you persecuted my people that flowed in my river of power. But my power is not bound. My power works and fights with my Word (Sword of the Spirit). They are immutable and can not be stopped, can not be hindered. Because, as long as the earth remains, I will have a mouth piece standing bold before me.

We already know that religious spirits will not embrace the supernatural power of God. That religious spirit likes for cute little God to stay in His place, cute little Jesus to stay in His place, and precious little Holy Spirit to stay in His place. When you talk about healing and deliverance and God forbid, don't open your mouth about speaking in tongues: this upsets religious folks. They feel you are out of control when you talk in your heavenly language. And they are right! You are out of control!! You're out of control of the human mind and all that is natural. You are flowing in the Holy Ghost, the Supernatural power of the Living God. Totally out of your control! This river is yet going to rise just like God showed Ezekiel. It will rise into an overflow. You can't damn Him up. No walls can contain Him! Just can not, just can not!

— *Rev. Dr. Janie Watkins* —

We will walk together carrying the banners of Jesus, declaring He is Lord! And, where ever Jesus is exalted, guess what? You will then find the mighty power of the Holy Ghost! Regardless of what you go through, exalt Jesus! If you don't exalt Him, the rivers wont flow. Remember, the rivers follows the Name of Jesus.

As in Ezekiel, if you're ankle, knee, or waist deep, you can't flow. You still have not relinquish control of your life to Jesus. But give total control to Jesus, that's when you will flow in the Super Natural. If you're at the controls, you may be in the flow, but the flow of God wont be in you. Don't fear what man can do to you, you must walk with Jesus. Don't be double- minded, reaching for Jesus with one hand, yet with the other hand, reaching for this world's system. He will not flow in you, if you do that. Wake up child of God. This is the hour of deliverance. Not tomorrow, not next week, but this is the hour to flow in God. The Holy Spirit is speaking with tongues all over the place. Yes, the rivers are flowing, get into the waters. As you move into the flow of the Holy Spirit, you might as well face it, there are some folks in your sanctified church that don't want to step out into these waters. They don't want to be baptized in the Holy Ghost and don't like it when you come in speaking in tongues as the Spirit of God gives utterances.

They haven't been baptized in the Holy Ghost and don't want you to be either. But, you have no choice, you know too much about Him.

This is God's desire for us. We must come "UP" in Him. That's the problem with majority of the "Body" today.

They've gotten stagnated instead of flowing in God. Waters that stands still will soon "Stink." And as it stinks, it draws types of bugs and creepy crawley things that hangs around stink things. You know what? There are people like that. They are satisfied with their "Traditional Religion." It's a bad thing when you're satisfied on this journey. Child of God, you must desire greater things in God. Don't ever be satisfied with just enough of God to keep you out of hell and the lake. You miss sooo much when you're satisfied. Always search for higher dimensions in Jesus. There are so many different Anointings and there are many levels of Anointings. Our God is so Vast, He can not be measured. And, this vast God of Glory has so much for us. Just come on in and sup with Him. Just flow in the Holy Ghost. Then and only then will you define your Purpose. (Your reason for being).

CHAPTER 7

HE'S ALREADY DEFEATED!!!

Yes, he's already defeated! (Luke 10:19) Jesus said, " I know he's defeated, because I saw him fall, and when he fell, it was like lightning. When he fell, he fell in authority, and he fell in power. But as Jesus exhaled, He said, But, I have given you power over all of his power. The King James translation does not give the clarity we need to adequately understand what Jesus was talking about. In the original Greek, this verse reads: He gave them Authority (Greek = Exeusia) over satan's power (Greek = Dunamus). Therefore, that verse should read: I have given you authority over all the authority of the enemy, to overcome all the power of the enemy.

When we get to the place where we realize the authority and power Jesus gave us, we will immediately go to another level in God. Once we understand "authority" here, we will know and understand that it's not power we need. We have that already. We just need to understand the authority we have been given. Authority is defined as permission given to us. Power is defined as Ability. We have to walk in the reality of Authority. Keep in mind that the enemy of your soul has limited power. The Holy Scriptures tells us that Jesus crushed his head. When you deal with the "head," you are dealing with the ability to think, the ability to reason. When Jesus crushed his head, he spoiled principalities and powers. He made an open shew of them Triumphing over them. (Col. 2:15), " and having spoiled principalities and powers, he made a shew of them openly, triumphing over them."

You see, your enemy knows better than you do, of your power. And, he definitely knows about your authority. It's the area of authority where he fights you the most. he does not want you to realize your authority in Jesus. If you realize your authority, he will do all he can to plant fear so you won't "walk" in authority. If you walk in fear, you'll never be in the position to make the defeated on put your stuff back. Christians have no reason to walk in fear, especially when you know who you are and who's you are. Once you realize who and who's you are, you will never fear again.

Remember I said earlier that Jesus crushed the devil's head. Well, that word, "crush" is defined as: to crash, to bruise, to break with force; to put out of shape; to ground or to pound into small bits, severe pressure, to subdue; to utterly defeat, to force down. This is what Jesus did to satan as He crushed the devil's head. He ground his thinking capacity into small bits. Jesus utterly defeated him. Jesus forced him down. This is why his way of thinking is twisted, his skull has been crushed, "Smile." Jesus Bruised his head, "smile." (Gen. 3:15), " And I will put enmity (hatred) between thee and the woman, and between thy seed and her seed; it shall bruise thy head, and thou shalt bruise his heel.

Jesus took authority from satan and gave it to us, "the Body of Christ." But in order to have totally authority over our enemy, we must be totally in submission to God. The Apostle James stated in (James 4:7), " Submit yourselves therefore to God, resist the devil and he will flee from you. Total submission to Christ Jesus, gives us complete jurisdiction, power, and authority over our enemy.

The basis then for walking in power and authority with God, is complete obedience to our God. This is where lucifer faltered. Instead of obeying God, he thought he was as good as God and said to himself: (Isaiah 14:14), " I will ascend above the heights of the clouds; I will be like the most High. How can the creature go above it's creator? Even the fact that he "thought" that he could do this, shows that he's walking in illegitimate authority. That's the problem with some of the "Body."

Susie and Carol, I will call them, (not their real names, but the story is true). Carol has been saved about two years and says that God called her into the ministry. She joined this church and is now preaching less than one year. Her pastor is trying to lead her the right way, yet she will not come under the authority of her pastor. So, she left, saying he's trying to hold her back. You know as well as I that he's only trying to steer her in the right direction so she won't be out there illegitimately. If a preacher is "Out there, out of joint, under no authority, no accountability to any one. They are walking in the Gospel illegally. God did not sanction that, and God will not bless that. Subsequently, the people that falls under this ministry will end up the same as she. Out of Joint and out of Order. What God Sanctions, He blesses. He will obligate Himself to bless it. So much for Carol. Now, Susie: Saved about five years, preaching three years. Yet, she like Carol, is now an authority on God. This is another one, out of joint and our of order. When God placed her under a ministry but she didn't go there because it's a large church. She can't easily be seen and heard there. So, she in turn goes and joins this smaller ministry so she can be seen and heard. Not caring that God didn't send her there. In fact, sometimes folks lie and say God said thus and so in order to justify why they do things. You see, the devil will always offer you a counterfeit. This is why it's so important for us to be sensitive to the Holy Spirit. It's critical that we know His voice from the voice of error.

The devil, when he was lucifer, the Word of God said, "he sealeth up the sum." (Ezekiel 28:12-15), " *Son of man, take up a lamentation upon the king of Tyrus, and say unto him, thus saith the Lord God; thou sealeth up the sum, full of wisdom and perfect in beauty. Thou has been in Eden, the garden of God; every precious stone was thy covering, the sardius, topaz, and the diamond the beryl, the onyx, and the jasper, the sapphire, the emerald, and the carbuncle, and gold: the workmanship of thy tabrets and of thy pipes was prepared in thee in the day that thou wast created. Thou art the anointed cherub that covereth; and I have set thee so: thou wast upon the Holy mountain of God; thou has walked up and down in the midst of the stones of fire. Thou wast perfect in thy ways from the day that thou wast created, til iniquity was found in thee."*

So you see, the devil (better than we) knows the ways of God. The "seal" is a keeper. The "Sum" are God's ways. he kept God's ways, he watched over God's ways. That's why he can so cleverly imitate God, he knows His ways.

He said, "I will be like the most High. So he knows how to look like God, sound like God, and make situations appear as though God has something to do with them. When behind the scenes, it's the devil that's controlling the puppet strings and making it "appear" that God is doing this. What ever you do, don't be like Carol or Susie. Walk in God's Order. Don't be a rebel out here on your own without a spiritual covering.

Because if you do, everything you preach and teach may sound good and look good, but it will still be out of order because you're out of order. You will not walk in God's authority and power, if you're out of order. The evil one seizes every moment to destroy you. he doesn't care how he go about it, he just want there to be nothing left of you. Jesus reminded Peter of this same thing when He told him that satan wanted to sift him as wheat. (Luke 22:31- 32), " *Simon, Simon, behold satan hath desired to have you, that he may sift you as wheat: But I have prayed for thee that thy faith fail not: And when thou art converted, strengthen thy brethren."* So if the devil wants to destroy you, certainly, he wants to take from you. And he has taken, and taken, and taken from you. Not only you, but generations before you. Your grandmother, your mother, and if you check into it, he's already started "taking" from your children and grandchildren (generations after you). The cycle "Must" be stopped. Will you be the one to stop satan in your family? Will you? Somebody in the bloodline's got to realize that he is already defeated! Why let someone that is already defeated, defeat you???

When you are converted, or when you have changed your mind about allowing the devil to keep taking from you, then you go up the ladder and take back what was taken from generations before you. And, you go and strengthen the generation that's after you so that this cycle can be broken. This is what Jesus was saying to Simon Peter. Go and strengthen your brother so he can see the illegal light too, and do something about it.

THE STRATEGIES OF THE evil one

The Holy Scriptures clearly defines satan's ways of working are through Temptation, Deception, and Accusation. The first thing he chooses to do is tempt us. This is what he did in Eden. he can not make us sin, but he tempts us to sin. But, Jesus established our authority against the devil as the tempter, when Jesus was in the wilderness. The devil's second way of pulling us down is through deception. The Word of God says, If it were possible, he would fool the very elect. (Matt. 24:24), " For there shall arise false christs, and false prophets, and shall show great signs and wonders; insomuch that if it were possible, they shall deceive the very elect.

He didn't say it was impossible to fool the very elect, He said, "If it were possible, they shall deceive the very elect. HEAR ME CHILD OF GOD! Jesus went on to say in verse 25-26, *"Behold, I have told you before. Wherefore if they shall say unto you, He is in the desert, go not forth; behold He is in the secret chambers;* believe it not. Do you see it? We must be sensitive to the voice of the Holy Spirit. Know His voice. Jesus said, my sheep know my voice. Get to know His voice. When you stay in His presence, you get to know His voice. And when you know His voice, you will not follow any other voice.

The third strategy satan uses is accusation. The Word of God declares him to be the accuser of the brethren. he goes before the Almighty day and night accusing us to God. (Rev. 12:10), *" And I heard a loud voice saying in heaven Now is come salvation and strength, and the kingdom of our God, and the power of His Christ: for the accuser of our brethren is cast down, which accused them before God day and night."*

Let me share something with you about the devil's accusations: There is power in his accusations. he is spirit and everything he does is spiritual. As in the spirit, so in the natural. he will "insinuate" something in "your mind" and twist his insinuations as though they are "your thoughts." This is how he builds strongholds in the mind.

Remember the chapter, "From Foothold to Stronghold? Not only will he accuse you "through you," he will use people to accuse you. But sometimes you may have to talk to yourself and deliver yourself from people. When I say "people," I'm talking about folks that say they are born again.

Again, satan's accusations are powerful. They are powerful only if we receive them. If we don't receive them, they bounce back to him. But if we receive them, they bring with them fear and discouragement. And, the next thing you know, you've lost your confidence in God (your only help). (Hebrews 10:35), " Cast not away therefore your confidence, which hath great recompense of reward." Yes, we will be rewarded or compensated a glorious reward just for having confidence in God.

In order to stop satan's accusations, just simply don't receive them. When he bring fear, quote the Holy Scriptures concerning fear. If you can't quote it, then look it up in the Bible and read it to him OUT LOUD! After you read to the devil, you meditate on what you read. Yes, get that Word in your spirit. Deposit the Word of God in your heart often enough, the mouth will speak it. Remember, out of the abundance (where there is a lot of it) of the heart, the mouth will speak. The pharisees constantly accused Jesus, but He refuted their words with the Word of God. He did not receive not even one accusation because they were all lies against His character. Even, and especially in the churches today, you will find so-called brothers and sisters accusing one another. This is the satanic work of the evil one. But we must submit to God's way of thinking, resist the devil and he has no choice but to flee. Whatever the devil brings to you, always keep in mind that he is a liar and he is already defeated. he has a destiny already "SET" for him. The lake of fire is his destiny. he's in chains and limited by God. Like I said, he's defeated!

I'm going to share this with you. It's fixed. God has fixed all things in eternity past. Isaiah spoke of lucifer (Isaiah 14:12), "as causing the nations to tremble. Ahhhh, but Jesus came and spoiled principalities, took power and authority away, and gave it to us, the Church. All of Heaven and all of hell knows the reality of that victory. O yes, devils know that they have an appointed "time" to walk in their destiny. That's why they asked Jesus, why have you tormented us before the time? They knew and they still know who Jesus is. They also know who we are. (Matt. 8:29), " And behold, they cried out saying, what have we to do with thee Jesus, thou son of God? Art thou come hither to torment us before the time?" Oh, they know Jesus and they know that they have a destiny. Child of God, we must recognize that the devil's defeated.

WHO IS THIS THAT HAVE MY STUFF?

The Holy Scriptures depicts him as a liar and the father of lies. The word of God in *John 8:44*, gives us part of his dossier. *"Ye are of your father the devil, and the lust of your father ye will do. he was a murderer from the beginning, and abode not in the truth, because there is no truth in him.*

When he speaketh a lie, he speaketh of his own: for he is a liar, and the father of it." At one time he had power from God, but he wanted to dethrone God and enthrone himself. he was then cast out of Heaven (Isa. 14:12). We must make sure we don't fall into what satan fell into. It's critical that we know where he's been, where he is now, and where he's going. (Eze. 28:14- 19), *"Thou art the anointed cherub that covereth; and I have set thee so: thou wast upon the Holy mountain of God; thou hast walked up and down in the midst of the stones of fire. Thou wast perfect in thy ways from the day that thou wast created, til iniquity was found in thee. By the multitude of thy merchandise, they have filled the midst of thee with violence, and thou hast sinned: therefore I will cast thee as profane, out of the mountain of God: and I will destroy thee, O covering cherub, from the midst of the stones of fire. Thine heart wast lifted up because of thy beauty, thy hast corrupted thy wisdom by reason of thy brightness: I will cast thee to the ground. I will lay thee before kings, that they may behold thee. Thy hast defiled thy sanctuaries by the multitude of thine iniquities, by the iniquities of thy traffik; therefore will I bring forth a fire from the midst of thee, it shall devour thee, and I will bring thee to ashes upon the earth in the sight of all them that behold thee. All they that know thee among the people, shall be astonished at thee; thou shalt be a terror, and never shalt thou be anymore."*

Iniquity was found in him because he wanted to exalt himself above God. he betrayed God! he was at one time, beautiful. God formed music in him, and placed a desire in him to worship God, and he led all the other angels into worship of God too. But he rebelled and wanted to be positioned as God! God did not tolerate his rebellion. God immediately cast him out of Heaven.

You see, lucifer knew all there was about praise and worship, as he was the Worship "Leader" in Heaven. satan wants our worship. When we worship God, we embarrass him before his devils, because he swares out that he is going to be worshiped instead of God. That's his ultimate goal, to be worshiped by us. his desire is not to get us to sin, but to get us to worship him. he bargained with Jesus in (Matt. 4:8-9), " Again, the devil taketh him up into an exceeding high mountain, and sheweth him all the kingdoms of the world and the glory of them; and saith unto him, all these things will I give thee, if thou will fall down and worship me." he lost with Jesus, but he's still trying to get us to worship him. lucifer had to have been given awesome authority in "Position" for him to even "think" that he could become equal with God. The position had to be high in power and authority because he was allowed to cause one-third of the angelic host to rebel with him. (Rev. 12:4- A), "And his tail drew the third part of the stars of Heaven, and did cast them to the earth. he had much, but lost it all when he tried to replace God in Heaven. When he was cast out of Heaven, he had and still have the "same" mentality. he tempted Eve by causing her to disobey God and eat of the tree of the knowledge of good and evil. he accused God of lying about the consequences of disobedience. And he deceived Eve, and through that deception, we all came under the Adamic curse. But, as we "obey" Jesus, we are delivered from this curse.

As we obey God's Word, our Victory is declared. Obedience to God is our victory against "every strategy" of the enemy. As we submit ourselves to God, when we resist the devil, he sees the face of Jesus on our face. This causes him to flee. When he sees us in submission to God, he sees absolute submission of Jesus to God the

Father. he can not stay around that kind of power, he knows that submission and obedience to God is an awesome power. We are to be Christ-like. We are to walk the way He walked and talk the way He talked. He called those things that were not, as though they were.

We have been given authority to overcome the devil. When we, as children of God, grasp this concept, we're on our way. Again, (*Luke* 10:19). When we receive this Scripture in our spirit, the defeated one will know that he's in trouble. When we give place to the devil, (believe his lies), we enthrone him in our lives. (E*ph*. 4:27), " *Neither give place to the devil.*"

We must "will" to give place "Only" to God. He created us with our own individual "will." He wants us to love and obey Him on purpose. When He breathe the breath of life in Adam, he then became a living soul. The soul consist of your "will, intellect, and emotion." When we choose to obey God over our own "will," we are then established by God in authority over the enemy. Deposit that in your spirit, child of God!

The whole issue here is "Authority," not "Power." This has been the issue from the time he tried to dethrone God, until he is cast into the lake of fire. And, he's going there, Yessssssss, he's going there.

This is still the issue today, when we are going through spiritual warfare. The question is, "WHO IS IN CHARGE?" Anytime when there's warfare, this is always the issue. Even in "natural" warfare. In Old Testament times, when kings would defeat another kingdom, they would stripped that defeated king naked, put him in bondage (tie his hands), and parade him down the streets so everybody could see that the king that's in bondage is no longer in charge. I remember reading in (I Sam. 3:10). In the battle against the Philistines, , when Saul's sons, Jonathan, Abenedab, and Malchi-Shura were killed. Saul was so badly wounded, he tried to get his armor bearer to kill him. He knew that if the Philistines found him half dead, they would abuse him and he could do nothing about it. His armor bearer would not kill him, so he killed himself. But, the Philistines, the next day came looking over the spoils and found Saul and his sons bodies among the dead. They cut off Saul's head and stripped him of his armor, and they let this be known among the people, that

Israel was no longer in charge, the Philistines were. They put Saul's armor in the house of ashtaroth, and nailed his headless body to the wall of Beth-shan. You see, the enemy's soul "purpose" is being "in charge," and he advertises that he's in charge.

But, he's not in charge. Jesus is in charge. He always have been and He always will be. Jesus is the First and the Last. It's common to hear Him referred to as the second Adam. If there's a second Adam, then there can be a third, fourth, and so on. But the Word of God declares Him to be the "Last Adam." (I Cor. 15:45), " And so it is written, the first man Adam was made a living soul; the last Adam was made a quickening spirit."

PRAISE AND WORSHIP STOPS HIM

The "Body" has got to wake up and realize that our

enemy is defeated. Yes, he still attacks us, but, we have an awesome arsenal of weapons that we're to use in his attacks. Are you aware that praise and worship is a weapon? It's an awesome weapon against the defeated one. There were many battles won in Old Testament times by the singers and praisers going ahead of the warriors. Oftentimes, it bought confusion to the enemy. Another example of praise and worship: When Paul and Silas was in prison. They prayed, and then they begin to worship God. The earth quaked as God came in. Remember, He inhabits (lives in) the praises of His people. We must "Tap in" to this. Through praise and worship, God causes fortified cities and kingdoms to fall. If we have footholds and strongholds in our hearts, through praise and worship, they must come down.

Like I said earlier, satan desire that we worship him. Even if he can't get us to worship him, he'll be satisfied if he can divert our worship to anything other than God. Oftentimes, when believers talks about worship, they refer to hands lifted, or lying prostrate, or bowing before the Lord. But praise and worship are attitudes of the heart. There's an awesome power in worship, and it's predicated on a right relationship with God. Everybody can praise Him, but it takes a level of truth to worship Him. (John 4:23-24), " *But the hour cometh and now is, when the true worshipers shall worship the Father in spirit and in truth.*"This let us know that our life has to be right. We "must" walk in "Integrity" in or to walk in truth.

My Organization gives three annul functions. (Conference, Black-tie Affairs, and Power Prayer

Breakfasts). We've been doing this for seven years. From the date of inception, I saw another side of some preachers. I have never seen so many ministers of the Gospel, "NOT WALKING IN INTEGRITY." (When it comes to money, that it).

I have never been more embarrassed. Our President of Registration saw this, and she always looked up to preachers. But she see folks now in a different light. Some folks told her that they already paid. Some said, they were told that the price was less. Some said, they told me that they would be at the conference only for Saturday. There were so many stores. And they were all untrue. That's not good at all, it's just not good. Where is the integrity of the ministers of God?

Getting back to praise and worship. Our praise must be in conjunction with a life of integrity, or we can not enter in to worship Him. Praise and worship are weapons like you wouldn't believe. We need to establish God's authority in our lives. We do this by tearing down every altar in our heart that does not bow down to Almighty God. Yes, a lot of us often go down to the altar to worship God. But, we go down with altars that have been set-up in our hearts. We must rid ourselves of every altar. The job can be an altar. Husbands and wives can be an altar. Our children, our money, can be an altar. But we've got to get rid of it. (Ex. 34:12-14), " Take heed to thyself, lest thy make a covenant with the inhabitants of the land whither thou goest, lest it be a snare in the midst of thee: But ye shall destroy their altars, break their images, and cut down their groves: (high places).

For thou shalt worship no other god: for the Lord whose name is jealous, is a jealous God.

The altars must go, the high places must go. When we worship, we turn inward to God. His altar is our heart. He wants our undivided attention, and He wants our undivided affection too.

The defeated one is standing out front, and our stuff is behind him. We must strip him of his armor, tear down his altars; and make him put our stuff back. We can demand that he put it back! I heard Pastor Rod Parsley say this about his pastor, Pastor Sumerall: Pastor Sumerall was in Africa and the devil was showing his hand. When Pastor Sumerall was getting ready for bed one evening, the bed started jumping all over the room. I guess that was to put fear in him. Immediately, he started binding the devil. The devil left, but he left his bed in the middle of the room. He called the devil back to the room. He said: hey mr. devil, put it back!!! Put my bed back where you got it from!!!! And sure enough, the bed started shaking again until it shook itself back where it was. O' yes, we've got power and authority over the devil, so make him put it all back and make him put it back Now!!!! You better hear me child of God!!! he's already defeated! Remember, Jesus saw him fall!

THE DEFEATED ONE IS A PREDATOR

Webster defines predator as: blood thirsty, Carnivorous, preys on others. There are some folks walking in covenant with the devil against you. And, they are so-called christians. Some of them are preachers. They are predators waiting to destroy you. We inter-act daily with numerous people, but you've better be on guard as to who you're interacting with. All relationships are not set-up to benefit us. Some relationships should be avoided. I'm speaking from personal experiences. At one time, I took this woman to be my friend. Every time I called her, I felt drained. She felt she had to always set up a wall before we started talking. Right away, I could see the devil standing up. I did not give her reason to feel this way, but it just happened. Well, I got tired of it. But, one day, I found myself calling her again. (I was a glutton for punishment). But, I heard the Holy Spirit say: "Cut the relationship and do it now." This relationship was consuming all of my energy. I feel so much better for not even having to think about defending myself over something silly. Something that was being said by someone being used of satan. The

Holy Spirit gave me insight as to the demon spirit (predator) behind the conversations.

Like I said earlier, the defeated one cares less how he destroys you, he just want to destroy you. When you're involved in a relationship that's sapping your strength, even if it's family members, and often times, it is, cut them off! These folks are used of satan to rob you of your achievements or of what you plan to achieve. They don't have anything and don't want you to have anything- cut them off!!! If you don't cut them off, you will not walk in your full potential. It's silly to hold on to this type relationship. It's the predator, cut them off!!!! These are people that undermine and hinder your success, cut them off!!!! Jesus could not do any miracles in His own hometown. The people in His hometown had such limited vision of Him. Their thoughts of Him was that He was the carpenter's son.

They played with Him when they were kids, or their children played with Him. Here He's talking about raising the dead, making blind men see. Healing people that were born crippled. People that were born deaf or dumb, he's talking about restoring their healing and speech. That's absurd. This is unheard of. They kept referring to Him as the carpenter's son, not knowing or caring to know that He was the Son of the Living God! Don't let people hold you back in the past. "They knew you when." Yes, but this is now, and you are not the same person. When people see you moving ahead of them, they want to keep you in the past. God has much for us, but we've got to move beyond the times past. That's just what they are: the times past. If you want to move forward in God, you can't keep going in the past, you've got to move forward.

There are some folks that are close to you, they are your main predators. Family members, church family members, and co-workers, etc. I've had co-workers to smile in my face and complement me. Yet, behind my back, they Sabotaged my work. It had gotten to a point that I had to make copies of everything I did and take the copies home. There are family members and church family members that are malicious manipulators, CUT THEM OFF!!!!! YOU BETTER HEAR ME! CUT THEM OFF!!!! If you plan to excel in God and anything else, you'd better cut them off!!! I know it sounds easy for me to say cut them off! But, I'm speaking from "personal" experience. When you are around people that you know are not for you, in fact you know they are against you, because they have proven to you time and time again that they are not with you. You don't just keep holding on to that type of relationship. Choose friends in people that are on a higher level than you are. Because, on your level is where you share your ideas. But, it's on your level where you find folks are constantly competing with you. It's on your level that folks are threatened by your success, and they try to do you in. So what you do is go to a higher level of folks that have already stepped into their purpose. They are not in the least threatened by your success. When you're in an atmosphere of people of this sort, your head is clear. You can now see your way clear to walk in your purpose.

Now, if there are family members or friends that you feel the relationship can be salvaged, then you must confront them on the issues that are troubling you. If they insist on being difficult, CUT THEM OFF!!!!! Even if you are tempted, don't go back into the relationship. (Prov. 26:11), " As a dog returneth to his vomit, so a fool returneth to his folly."

Get a grip on your own life and stop allowing other people to manipulate your feelings. You take total control, for it's **your life.** It's **your Purpose.** Don't allow anyone to side-track you. Always keep in mind, it's not the person that's scheming against you to prevent you, it's the predator, the evil and defeated one. But, stay focused, because Jesus has given us power and authority over all the power and authority of the evil one. Stay focused. Command the defeated one to put your stuff back! PUT IT "ALL" BACK AND PUT IT BACK RIGHT NOW!!!!!!!!

FOR ADDITIONAL COPIES WRITE:

NATIONAL CONFERENCE OF
MEN/WOMEN IN MINISTRY
P.O. BOX 20956
PHILA., PA. 19141

AVAILABLE AT YOUR LOCAL BOOKSTORE OR YOU MAY ORDER DIRECTLY FROM THE ADDRESS ABOVE OR CALL: (215) 224-5703.
WE ACCEPT VISA, MASTERCARD, DISCOVER AND AMERICAN EXPRESS.

EXCEPTIONALLY ANOINTED MESSAGES
"2 AND 4 TAPE SERIES PACKAGES"

A. IT'S A "WOMAN" THING
Send For The Mourning Women
The Office Of The Midwife

B. IT'S NOT "YOUR" FIGHT
The Battle Is The Lord's
It's A Fixed Fight

C. I'M JUST "BLESSED"
You Can't Curse What God Has Blessed
Blessed Beyond Measure

D. THE "JESUS" ISSUE
Who Is This Jesus?
Jesus Of Nazareth
The Ministry Of Jesus
In The "Name" Of Jesus

E. RELEASE IT!
Let It Go, I
Let It Go, II

F. SPLIT TONGUES
Tongues Of Fire, I
Tongues Of Fire, II

Two-Tape Series . . . . *Gift Of $12* + $2.50 s&h
Four-Tapes Series . . . . *Gift Of $24* + $5.00 s&h

MY GIFT IN SUPPORT OF THE MINISTRY

*"As God strengthens Janie Watkins Ministries,
we are determined to make a difference in the lives of others."*

Yes, Dr. Watkins, I want to help your ministry "heal" broken lives.
Enclosed is my additional gift of:

❏ $10   ❏ $15   ❏ $20   ❏ $_____

Product Total (from previous page): $_____
Gift Total (above): $_____
   Total Enclosed: $_____

CREDIT CARD GIVING
Please charge my order and gift to my:

❏ Visa ❏ Master-Card   ❏ Discover   ❏ AmEx

Acct.No._____

Exp. Date____ /____ Phone (_____)_____

_____
Print your name above as it appears on your card

_____
Authorized Signature

PLEASE MAKE CHECKS OR MONEY ORDERS PAYABLE TO: JANIE
WATKINS MINISTRIES
P.O. BOX 20956
PHILADELPHIA, PA 19141

CASSETTE TAPE SELECTION BY REV. JANIE WATKINS

1. A New Thing
2. The Harvest
3. Church Protocol
4. Let It Go, I (series)
5. Jesus of Nazareth
6. The Battle Is The Lord's
7. Tongues Of Fire, I (series)
8. Outside Of The Camp
9. Get In Position
10. The Potter's House
11. Liberated To Serve
12. Praying To Get Results
13. Tongues of Fire, II (series)
14. The Office Of The Midwife
15. Learning To Pray
16. The Ministry Of Jesus
17. The Foolish Churchgoer
18. I Am And I Will
19. The Fires Of God
20. Let It Go, II (series)
21. Discerning The Spirit Of A Matter
22. You Can't Curse What God Has Blessed
23. It's A Heart Thing
24. The Gifts Of The Holy Spirit (series)
25. Where Are You?
26. The Secret Place
27. There's a "Set Time" in God
28. The Manifested Dream
29. Blessed Beyond Measure

30. The Most High God
31. The Bible Taught B From Genesis to Revelation
32. If It's Dead, Deal With It
*33. It's Time To Bind And Loose
34. In The "Name" Of Jesus
35. Soaring With Eagle
36. Call For "The Mourning Women"
37. He Heard My Cry
38. Guard Your Anointing
39. The Third Person
*40. It Just Don't Make No Sense
41. It's A "Fixed Fight" (series)
42. Be Of One Mind
43. The Spirit Of Jezebel
44. There's a Cool Wind A Blowing
45. Beauty For Ashes
46. Shaking, But The Power Is Gone
47. Soaring With Eagles
*48. Let's Get Loosed
*49. I Can't Stoop That Low
*50. Let's Get High

* Not Yet Duplicated

Video : Guard Your Anointing $10.
Cassettes PRICED $5. each
Cassette Albums $12